THINGS THAT MY FATHER FORGOT TO TELL ME

THINGS THAT MY FATHER FORGOT TO TELL ME

A letter to Teenagers and Adults Who Seek the Wisdom of the Elders

John Chitakure

THINGS THAT MY FATHER FORGOT TO TELL ME
A letter to Teenagers and Adults Who Seek the Wisdom of the Elders

Copyright © 2019 John Chitakure. All rights are reserved. Except for brief quotations in critical publications or reviews, no part of this book may be reproduced in any manner without prior written permission from the author. Write: John Chitakure, 3718 Southern Grove, San Antonio, TX 78222, USA. Email: jchitakure@gmail.com.

PAPERBACK ISBN: 978-0-9998339-2-6

Published by John Chitakure. San Antonio, Texas, USA

*To all single mothers,
for their courage and wisdom in raising their kids,
and to all orphans,
who never had an opportunity to learn about life from their parents,
but still make it in life.*

Contents

Preamble----------------------------------3

Introduction------------------------------6

Self-Discipline--------------------------12

Political Involvement--------------------35

Friendship-------------------------------49

Generosity and Gratitude-----------------60

Decision-Making--------------------------73

The Importance of Education--------------81

Enmity-----------------------------------88

Cultural Diversity-----------------------96

Summing it Up--------------------------- 104

Preamble

In 2012, my family and I miraculously got Diversity visas to become permanent residents of the United States. Although this acquisition could have been a welcome miracle to most people in my situation, it wasn't easy for me to make the decision to leave Zimbabwe: my extended family, friends, job, and home, and wade into the unknown American cultural waters. I knew that there were challenges awaiting us in the USA because I had lived there for a couple of years before. We would be vulnerable aliens in a foreign land where racism is still an issue to be dealt with. However, for the sake of the future our children, and the unending harassment from Zimbabwe's economic meltdown, my wife and I braved the winds, and came to the United States. Yes, there were challenges that we encountered as chronicled in my recent memoir, *The Audacity to Dream: Stories from an African Immigrant*, 2018, but our will to survive was far greater than our discomfort. Yes, we survived. The kids are now in college, and my wife and I are working. We will forever be grateful for the assistance we received from friends and the American people.

We have had our fair share of challenges too. One of the things that I quickly missed here (USA), particularly for the benefit of our boys, was the presence of the so many informal teachers to educate our kids about life. In Zimbabwe, teachers of our cultural norms, personal character, and discipline were ubiquitous. Every elder had a role to play. We had uncles, aunts, teachers, friends, and neighbors who could teach our kids about our values and norms.

In Zimbabwe, our kids were in a boarding school where they could learn many things about life from their peers. In the United States, it would be different since making friends wouldn't be easy for them. American kids keep to themselves because they have been taught to stay away from strangers for good reasons. They call it, "stranger, danger."

When we arrived here in the United States in 2012, I thought that Americans didn't have kids. There were no kids playing on the streets or even in front yards of the houses of their parents, as they would normally do in Zimbabwe. I saw no kids riding bikes on the same streets. Later, I was enlightened by our host. Kids were playing inside their parents' houses. They couldn't be outside alone because someone could snatch them away. It was a very surprising and saddening reality. So, kids had their childhood stolen from them by some creepy adults. Kids couldn't be kids in America because someone out there was waiting to pounce on them. That's not the end of the story; I was told not to look at kids as if I liked them because that's one of the telltales of pedophiles. So, our boys wouldn't only be deprived of the wisdom of the elders, but also that of their peers.

We also soon discovered that it's the responsibility of parents to teach their own kids about life. That wasn't new to us. We knew that we would do our best to teach them, but there were certain things that we wouldn't feel comfortable discussing with the boys. There would be things that we didn't know. Also, there would be things that we would forget or had no time to teach them. That's where the idea to write them this letter originated.

This letter is a result of my reflection on my personal life experiences, and I started writing it in 2012. My intention is to make this letter as original as possible. Any resemblance to any written works or ideas may be a result of life experiences being similar. I avoided consulting books already written so that I could present my ideas as mine. However, life experiences involve several aspects—mistakes, blessings, readings, education, interaction with others, and it's true that we gather our wisdom from all of them. Although I vouch for the originality of my ideas, I would be too myopic and naïve to think that no one else has ever had similar experiences and ideas.

Although my original idea was to write this letter for my boys only, I later changed my mind because there are many young people in Zimbabwe and perhaps in other countries, who are exactly in the same place as my children. Such children and their parents will immensely benefit from a letter of this nature. Therefore, this letter is for everyone—teenagers, parents, teachers, pastors, and counselors. It doesn't only refresh one's memories about the things one was taught, but it also explores and offers some new perspectives of looking at life experiences, and what can be learnt from them.

Every chapter starts with a couple of Shona proverbs, and their English translations. The Shona proverbs contain the traditional wisdom of the Shona elders. They were composed out of the experiences that the people had, and can be applied to the present life experiences of the readers because of their philosophical and didactic nature.

John Chitakure, San Antonio, Texas, USA (March 17, 2019)

Introduction

Kuziva mbuya huvudzwa (People get their knowledge from education).
Chawawana batisisa, mudzimu haupi kaviri (A person should make good use of the opportunities and privileges that he or she has).
Akuruma nzeve ndewako (The person who gives you advice is your friend).
Zano ndega akasiya jira mumasese (A person who refuses to get advice from others, often gets into serious trouble).

My sons, I have always wanted to sit down with you and discuss the challenges, joys, sorrows, mysteries, secrets, and vicissitudes of human life. I always hoped that I could spare some time to lecture you about the noble pursuit of good behavior and character (*unhu*). I have always wanted to share with you the grains of wisdom that I have acquired from my life experiences—failures and successes, losses and blessings, and weaknesses and strengths. They say that wisdom comes with age, and I consider myself old and wise enough to be able to share a little wisdom with you.

Of course, boasting isn't a virtue. I don't claim to have gained the amount of wisdom that's proportionate to my age. However, I profess to have acquired enough wisdom to be able to share some of it with you. Despite my noble hopes, I haven't been able to give you such a valuable lesson about life, up to now, because of several reasons.

First, both of us have no time to sit down and talk. We are too busy. On my part; I spend most of my time at work where I try to impart my wisdom unto my students, some of whom, rarely appreciate those noble efforts. It's true that time has become scarce. Our society has economically retrogressed to the old days when our people were hunters and gatherers, and because of that they were always on the move in pursuit of food and other necessities of life. We no longer own our time because it belongs to our employers, in exchange for a few dollars every week or month. It doesn't matter how hard and how long we work, we don't seem to get a fair remuneration. There were times when workers looked forward to the coming of the retirement age, but not now. Anyone considering retiring from work, might as well consider retiring from living. These days, workers try to postpone retirement as long as their employers can allow. Some work until the day they die. They do that, not because they are greedy, but because they never get enough reward to enable them to retire at the appropriate age without the risk of becoming destitute.

Time has become too scarce, my sons, as you shall discover when you join the wild goose chase of employment. On most working days, by the time I get back home, I am so exhausted that engaging in a serious conversation about the mysteries of life and the pursuit of wisdom is the last thing that I want to do. Discussing life drains a lot of energy, and I need to store enough energy for the next working week. We don't even own our own strength.

Looking at it from another perspective, it's good that humans don't have all the time in the world. If they had, the world would be more chaotic than it's right now. They say that idle minds are the devil's workshops. You can imagine what the devil can do if his messengers owned all the time in the world.

On your part, you are away from home most of the time. You spend most of your time at school with teachers and other strangers who have become a second family to you. Teachers are good and well-meaning people, most of the time, but they can't replace me, your father. Of course, most teachers are wiser than some parents, but nothing surpasses the wise words that have come from teachers but are delivered through the mouth of one's own father.

You don't have time, my sons, for you don't own the little time that you claim to be yours. When you come back home from school, you must perform the most important ritual of education that you call homework. There are times when I feel that this routine is overdone, and because of that, it may become detrimental to students' academic development. I am not complaining about the homework that's given in right dosages, and as a way of aiding and cultivating understanding in the student. What I find somehow repulsive is the homework that enslaves the student, parents, and most probably, the teacher who is obliged to prescribe and grade it. I give my students homework too, but not as a way to enslave or suffocate them with work, but to cultivate their academic growth.

Going back to the scarcity of time; the fact is that both of us can scarcely create enough time for an education of the type that I am proposing here. It's an education where you will neither be tested nor graded in the manner that you are used to. The testing and grading will be performed by life experiences and the society. You must realize that the education from life experiences takes a lifetime, because didactic experiences come when they want.

Second, you are still too young to understand the depth and the seriousness of the issues I want to talk to you about. I should wait, patiently. But patience as a virtue is more useful to immortal people than to transient beings. For some of us who started late in life and seem to live on borrowed time, the right time to do anything good is now. Waiting for tomorrow isn't good because tomorrow might never come or might come too soon. There were many fathers who wished to say one or two words of wisdom to their children, but they never had the opportunity to do so because death whisked them away too soon. Yes, death does that. My sons, I have nothing against being patient, but when patience turns into procrastination, then it's no longer a desirable virtue.

Third, some topics that I intend to discuss with you, my sons, are sensitive or even embarrassing between a father and his sons, yet they are crucial. If I don't talk about these topics with you now, then, you are bound to learn about them from other sources, and the chances of distortions are higher. So, although they are sensitive and embarrassing issues, you need to hear about them from me because real life knows no boundaries or embarrassment.

Fourth, there is too much contradicting information flying around, and that has become very confusing to any normal young person. The internet is awash with all sorts of information, which is a good thing. However, one of the greatest setbacks of internet information to young people is that some don't know how to select good and useful information from harmful and useless information. This letter, my sons, will suggest to you the direction you need to follow in your ongoing search for wisdom. Use my words as a compass that guides you towards the right destination but never as the destination itself. You use these words to manufacture your own wisdom, not as an end in themselves.

Finally, I have always feared to waste my time, trying to teach you something that you may not appreciate, now. The major challenge of education for life is that its necessity might not be appreciated until later when real life presents you with situations to which the knowledge that has been acquired from such an education can be applied. Education for life is hard to understand, and might not be taken seriously until one is in need. Because of your tender age, some things might be beyond your comprehension. So, you may not benefit from learning them now. Instead, I have decided to write this long letter rather than talking to you.

At first, when the idea of writing you a letter came to my mind, I was struck by the weirdness of a father writing a letter to the children with whom he shares a home. Be that as it may, I am now convinced that it's one of the best ways a father may communicate with his children.

There are many advantages that both of us will derive from this method of communication. First, this letter has the capacity to immortalize my words. You will always go back to it for more ideas whenever and wherever you need them. This letter will be like a spring of water to you because it will never run dry. Spoken words are quickly forgotten, but written words will live forever. You can also use it as a resource to teach the same, to your own children and your children's children. You may develop and expand some of my ideas as dictated by the amount and quality of wisdom that life would have bestowed on you.

In addition to the immortality of the written words, there are many boys who wished to learn about life from their fathers, but their fathers died before they could do that. Some fathers, just like I, are too busy to teach their children about life. My own father died when I was very young, and I practically learned nothing from him except what I genetically inherited from him. I wish he had written a letter. I got most of the wisdom that I claim to have from other boys' fathers, and at times, through the rough interactions I had with reality. Therefore, this public letter isn't only for you, my sons, but also for those who have no one to educate them about life.

Furthermore, there are many men of goodwill who desire to say one wise word to their sons, but unfortunately, they don't know where and how to begin. They don't have that talent, and we must appreciate the fact that people are different. They have different stations in life. Although all people claim to have wisdom, many of them don't know how they can impart it to their own children. There are many issues that I explore in this letter that will be of benefit to such parents. This public letter will be a resource to such fathers.

Moreover, our people have a proverb that says, "*Zvikomo zvinopanana mhute*" (Hills share their fog). Human beings share their knowledge and wisdom. Wisdom that isn't shared isn't wisdom at all. If people share their knowledge and wisdom, then we will end up having a world full of wise people. Smart people can survive any human or natural catastrophe. It's the lack of wisdom that drives people to hatred, war, xenophobia, racism, tribalism, corruption, oppression, dictatorship, abuse, greed, and many other societal ills. Please, share this letter with as many people as you can, so that they also benefit from my wisdom.

Another reason is that in Zimbabwe, and probably many other countries too, many men have gone into the diaspora in search of greener pastures, and many have left their children in the care of their wives and grandparents. Some of the immigrant workers go back home only once annually, and they don't have much time to interact with their kids. Most of them dedicate the little time they have in addressing other pertinent family issues. The children who have diasporic parents may also make use of this letter.

Finally, there are those many single mothers who stoically carry out the duties of both father and mother in their families. Most societies have great respect for such mothers, and the work they do for the society. They single-handedly raise their children, sometimes under very challenging conditions. As women, there are certain things that they might not understand about men, not because men are very sophisticated animals, but because one has to live with a man in order to understand him better. Of course, at times, men can be very difficult to comprehend, not because they can always wisely conceal their true characters, but because of their unpredictability. Sometimes, what men do is so shameful and embarrassing that no sane woman would try to understand it. Let those good mothers, who have become both mothers and *fathers* to their kids, benefit from a public letter of this nature— written, not by an angel or celebrity, but by just an ordinary and nameless mortal.

In conclusion, I would like to encourage you to take the words enshrined in this letter seriously, because if you follow them you will be transformed. They will enlighten and vivify you as young men, and will make you wiser when you become older. They will direct you to where more wisdom can be discovered. This wisdom will give you the food you will eat, the clothes you will wear, the house in which you will live, the friends who will accompany you in this life's journeys, the women who would become the mothers of your children, and most of all, the inspiration to live life to its fullest. Read it. Cherish it. Talk about it. Critique it. Understand it. Share it. However, this epistle isn't divinely inspired. It isn't infallible. You have no obligation to believe its contents. You may choose to learn from it or not. The choice is yours. But you have to read it first, for you to make that decision.

Self-discipline

Zingizi gonyera pamwe, maruva enyika haaperi (One shouldn't try to pursue all the pleasures of the world at once because they are endless).
Ramba kuudzwa akaonekwa nembonje pahuma (The one who doesn't give heed to discipline or advice will get into serious trouble).

My sons, at some point in the growing up of children, they sometimes harbor negative feelings towards their parents because of some of the responsibilities that our society has entrusted unto them as their guardians. As a man, I will write about the responsibilities of fathers. Fathers have many responsibilities that they should stoically, fervently, and unwaveringly shoulder for the benefit of their families and the society. They are expected to relentlessly enforce good and acceptable morals unto their children, at all costs. Yes, at all costs.

My sons, failure is never an option to any father. Every father, who is worth his salts endeavors to plant the seeds of self-control and self-discipline in his offspring. Sometimes, this sacred responsibility compels the father to discipline those children who aren't eager to observe the acceptable societal norms and morals. Self-control and self-discipline are neither easy to teach, nor comfortable to learn. Learning them involves the transformation of the learner, and that change is sometimes painful. Change challenges a person to let go the familiar old self in order to embrace the unfamiliar new self. However, whether you like learning self-control and self-discipline or not, there is one thing you must always bear in mind—that most fatherly discipline is never a result of hatred, but of love and respect for his children, and the society.

Every child is born like a wild animal, without any knowledge of what's allowed and disallowed by the society in which he or she is born. Hence, it becomes the duty of every parent to plant the seeds of societal norms and values in his or her children's hearts by means of training. Of course, it isn't an easy task for both the teacher and the disciple, but once the exercise is successfully completed, both the teacher and the disciple can look at each other and nod their heads in agreement that the bumpy journey was worth traveling together. There is nothing that gives a parent greater joy than witnessing his or her children becoming successful at school, workplace, and in the society. Conversely, there is nothing that pierces the heart of a parent deeper than witnessing one's children being taken to prison, failing to make it in life, or dying prematurely because of a lapse in their judgment. My sons, lessons in self-discipline and self-control are important. Usually, most children realize how vital and fruitful their lessons in self-discipline were after the teacher is long gone, and because of that they may not be able to express their gratitude to the teacher.

My sons, the teaching of self-discipline may be likened to how a driver can start a car that has a malfunctioning starter. The owner of the car that has that problem, sometimes with the help of neighbors or just passers-by, should push the car, in order to force it into generating its own motion. The push shouldn't be for a long distance, lest it becomes an unbearable burden for the car's owner and his helpers. The push must be harder and faster just before the car engine kicks into life. But once the car has started generating its own motion, the pushers must stop pushing it. The mission has been accomplished. Usually, at this point, the helpers stand, with arms akimbo, and feeling satisfied with a job fruitfully done. The driver and some of the pushers can now jump into the car and enjoy the ride to their destination. But, if the car fails to achieve that self-generated motion, during and after giving it a considerable push, they just leave it alone, for the time being, and device other ways of persuading it to generate its own motion. My sons, I want you to know that the objective behind pushing a car that has a defective starter isn't to punish it, but to give it the initial impetus that it needs to generate its own power and motion. Once it begins to move by itself, people should stop pushing it.

Self-discipline can be likened to the above analogy. It should be introduced to children in small doses starting from their tender ages, and then in bigger doses as the children reach their teenage years. It should be an on-going process until the child becomes an adult. No one wants to push a car with a defective starter forever. The push must come to an end at some point. Teaching children self-discipline shouldn't be a lifelong task for any parent; it should stop at a certain point. The older the child, the fewer, but deeper, the lessons he should receive.

My sons, when you were younger, I disciplined you more often because you hadn't mastered the techniques of engendering your own discipline. The discipline was intended to give you the impetus to produce your own discipline and self-control. The goal of disciplining children is to empower and encourage them to become the authors of their own destinies.

At times, I pushed you harder, and at other times, the push was gentler, but I must remind you that it was out of love. I don't want to push you forever. The pushing must come to an end at some point. Even if I wanted to push you forever, I wouldn't be able to do that because I am a mortal being. Mortals don't live forever. My sons, I want you to take that responsibility off my shoulders. I have done my job, and I have done it well. You should learn to discipline yourselves. Learn self-control. Be your own teachers. I can't be your teacher for all eternity. Don't hesitate to play your part.

Self-discipline is crucial to every man. A man without self-discipline is like a moving car without a driver. Worse still, he is like an airplane without a pilot. Such a car or plane isn't only a danger to itself and its passengers, but also to the rest of humanity. If you don't learn to make your own discipline now, you will regret it in life. Society would arrest you, take away all your freedom, potential, and happiness; and incarcerate you for several years, depending on the nature and magnitude of your indiscipline. You will go to prison, and you won't like it. When you come back from prison, you will never be the same. Society will strip you of your humanity and dignity. Many people who become victims of the prison system always regret the lost opportunity of learning self-discipline that their parents offered them to no avail.

Oh, yes. If you make a single mistake, society will take you to prison. When you come out of prison, society will magnify your single mistake, and pretend to forget all the good you would have done throughout your life. Yes, most societies are unforgiving to ex-convicts. Most societies subscribe to the fallacious philosophy that says, "Once a criminal, always a criminal." My sons, self-discipline is indispensable. There are several areas of human life that call for your unwavering self-discipline and self-control.

My sons, I want you to know that it's human to have sexual feelings and drives. Most human beings are sexual animals, in the sense that they are conjugally attracted to other people. Every man, sooner or later, must be called upon by the drives of his body to require sexual gratification. Even those men who might try to suppress such feelings because of the reasons best known to themselves, the need for conjugal gratification is bound to manifest itself in one way or the other. Sometimes, sexual desire demands recognition through unsolicited erotic dreams. You don't need to fear that. That's being human. No man should be afraid of being a man. Sexual drives are normal. However, sexual drives should be treated with extreme caution.

Although it's normal to have sexual feelings, and to need sexual gratification, sexuality is an area of every man's life that demands maximum self-discipline. I want you to know that wanting to have sex or fantasizing about it isn't a sin. It's part and parcel of being human. The creator God and ancestors are responsible for us having this precious, powerful, and mysterious aspect of our life. In fact, we should be grateful to the creator for making us sexual beings. However, unless you learn to control your sexual drives, they can be very destructive to both you and society. Sexual drives are like fire that can consume even the one who would have ignited it.

My sons, learn how to control your sensual drives. The major challenge about human sexual drives is that, they can only be controlled by their owner. No one else can control your sexual feelings for you. You are the only one who knows how gracious they are. It's you who know how compelling and enslaving they can be. Other people are only there to complement your efforts in either satisfying or domesticating them. The fight is huge. The first step is to own them. They are yours. The second thing is to understand them. They can be very complicated. And the third step is to control them. They can be very pushy and bully. The last step is to responsibly, respectfully, and legally indulge them. They can bring you much happiness.

You will fall in love with women, my sons. It's normal. You should realize that there are many types of women in this world: big and small, tall and short, cruel and kind, beautiful and ugly, loose and decent, but all of them are women. The choice is yours. Never be attracted to a woman only because of her outward appearance, for beauty deceives. Of course, there is nothing wrong with outward beauty, but be careful. Beauty shouldn't be the only aspect of a woman that attracts you. Choose character. If you go for character, you won't go wrong. Outward beauty may fade away, but character lives forever. If given a choice between beauty and character, please, go for character. Go for the beauty of the heart.

But remember, it's not easy to judge a woman's character. A woman's character isn't written on her forehead. You will have to discern it as you interact with her. Some women can hide their true characters until after your wedding. But after the wedding, it will be a little bit too late to escape the relationship. Of course, I don't have the formula for measuring a woman's character, therefore, I can't recommend one for you. Device your own methods. Whatever method you use, go for character, not for the looks. If you find a woman who possesses both beauty and character, don't hesitate to marry her because it doesn't happen all the time. My sons, I want you to know that a woman's physical appearance can be magnetic and hypnotizing to a man, but that doesn't make her a woman of character. When the physical beauty vanishes, as it sometimes does, and the hypnosis of infatuation is gone, your woman will remain with her character.

Character can be seen in little things that she does. The way she cares about herself, friends, and family members is crucial. If she doesn't take good care of herself, she may not be able to take care of you. It's easier to care for oneself than for another person. If she doesn't have empathy for other people, she may not have it for you when you need it most. If she doesn't respect herself and other people, she will disrespect you at a time when you need respect most. If she tells lies about other people, she will feed you with lies at a time when honesty can heal your heart's wounds. If she lacks kindness for other people, she will treat you the same when a little kindness is all that you need for healing and transformation. If she doesn't forgive other people, she will deny you forgiveness when just a handful of it can save your marriage. If she has no conviction about the things in which she believes, she may not be able to take a stance against the winds of temptations that will come in life. If she is greedy, she will try to make financial profit out of the union. If she is pompous, she will forsake important things in pursuit of vanity. My sons, it isn't easy to determine a person's character, but be on the lookout for some signs of its absence.

If you have an option to choose between the beauty of the heart and that of the face, please go for the heart. The beauty of the face may fade away, but a beautiful heart lives forever. The beauty of the face may be cosmetic, but no one can fake the beauty of the heart. The beauty of the face can be bought with money, but the beauty of the heart is generated from self-discipline. The beauty of the face may expire because of old age, but the beauty of the heart grows stronger with age. Go for character. Go for the heart. This advice doesn't mean that there are no beautiful women of good character. The world is full of them. Good luck!

In some cases, the beauty of the face overshadows the ugliness of the heart. Be cautious. If you find a woman who possess both beauty and character, buy her an airplane, and don't cease to thank God and the ancestors for leading her your way. Sometimes children look at their own mother, and wonder what could have compelled their father to marry her—it's her heart. Tell them; it's the beauty of her heart that counts.

Whatever type of women appeals to you, my sons, avoid sexual activities before marriage. Conjugal activities should wait for the wedding day because that's the ritual that gives you the certificate that you need to explore all the sexual mysteries that you ever fantasized about. Engaging in premarital sexual activities is like driving a car without a driver's license—the longer and more frequent you do it, the stronger you are convinced that a driver's license is unnecessary. An unlicensed driver isn't only a danger to the unfortunate car, but also to himself, his family, other drivers, and the society as a whole. Premarital sex, like any other stolen waters, is sweeter, but may be very costly. It may take away your peace of mind. It may cut short your bachelorhood. It may take away your freedom. Even if nothing happens to you because of it, it still isn't right.

My sons, respect all the women that you will meet in life. Treat them as if they were your mother or sisters. Most women may look invincible outwardly, but deep inside, they are as delicate as flowers. Don't deflower them. They may appear very loose and irreverent, but they are as sacred as temples. Don't desecrate them. Learn to respect all women because they are sacred vessels of their communities and families. Girls are the daughters of their parents. The same girls will be the wives of their husbands, and mothers to their children. Don't do to them what you wouldn't want anyone to do to your mother, sister, or daughter. Some of them might be immature and gullible, but please, don't take advantage of that.

If a woman disrespects you, or shouts at you without a cause, don't retaliate, but educate her with respect. Continue to respect her. If you are to reprimand a woman, do it with love and respect. If you are to divorce your wife, do it with respect. If your girlfriend abandons you for another man, don't shame and dehumanize her by sharing her secrets on the internet. Don't ever share her compromising pictures with other people because it reveals more about your immaturity than hers. All that was shared and done in confidence should remain like that forever. Don't ever blackmail your ex-girlfriend, for love can never be a result of blackmail.

My sons, open your hearts' ears for what I am about to say now. Never force yourself upon a woman. It doesn't matter how attractive, seductive, powerless, desperate, provocative, or vulnerable she might be; please, leave her alone. Never rape a woman, for it's shameful, inhuman, and criminal. Any unconsented sexual intercourse is called rape, if you didn't know. Any unwelcome touch, caress, hug, kiss, and patting, of a woman is an assault. Don't do it.

Of all sexual assaults, rape is the worst. Rape is a hideous and pernicious criminal offense in all human societies that possess a conscience. If you want to be intimate with a woman, ask for her consent.

Never imagine it. If a woman hugs and kisses you, don't assume that she wants to have sex with you. If a woman undresses herself, and lie on the bed by your side, that's not a license for you to abuse her. There is no silent and perpetual consent when it comes to sexual encounter—confirm it. Let "yes" be yes, and "no" be no. If possible, let it be in writing for every sexual encounter that you have outside of matrimony.

My sons, the abuse of a woman takes away the humanity of both the victim and the perpetrator. Abusing women turns the perpetrator into a wild animal. It turns you into a murderer. Yes, a rapist is a murderer. Rape kills the victim, many times after it's committed, as the victim continues to relive the horrendous violation of her body, throughout her life. A murderer who takes away a woman's life does it once, but a rapist kills the victim a thousand times. A rapist kills a woman's dignity, self-esteem, trust, love, and self-worth.

My sons, I want you to realize that your male organs were bestowed unto you for noble purposes, and not for raping women and men. Don't misuse them. Don't turn your male organs into weapons of both self and woman destruction. You need self-control. Many men who failed to control their sexual drives, and succumbed to their natural, but misdirected demands, found themselves in serious trouble. Some rapists are regretting that they were ever born. Yes, you may successfully rape a woman once or twice or even a few more times, but be rest assured that any forced sexual activity could be your last supper.

Yes, you may silence, threaten, or bribe the victim, but not forever. Most sex offenders end up in prison where their guaranteed right to marry is taken away by the State. Your right to marry and enjoy sexual relations won't be recognized or respected in jail. You may force a woman to be intimate with you once or twice, but your subsequent incarceration will deprive you of erotic intimacy for many years. Don't rape a woman. Discourage your friends from doing so. Don't waste your effort on a woman who doesn't want to be intimate with you because there are many women out there who are dying to surrender themselves to you lovingly, legally, and willingly.

Don't take pride in yourself because of the number of women you have bedded, deflowered, and abandoned, because that will count heavily against you in life. A man should be capable of controlling his sexual drives. For me, a real man is the one who can spend a whole night in a secluded place with a defenseless woman, and assures her of her sexual safety, to the extent that she can take off her clothes, and join that man in the same blanket, sleep soundly throughout the night, and wake up in the morning, to find her womanhood still unviolated. A real man doesn't take advantage of a sleeping woman. Only witches take advantage of sleeping people.

Of course, I don't suppose that to be easy, but it's the mark of a man, who is ruled by his conscience, and not by his manhood. The struggle is worth taking, even if it means spending the whole night in a battle for supremacy against one's treacherous and relentlessly begging manhood. The society counts on such men for the dignity and protection of our women and children. A man's worth isn't measured by the number of virgins he has deflowered, and women he has bedded, but by the number of girls whose virginity he has helped to preserve, and the vulnerable and unwilling women he has refused to bed. How would you feel if someone were to brag about having deflowered your sister or any other relative?

My sons, there is no difference between a man who can't control his sexual desires and a brute animal—a wild dog. If you aren't merciless and ruthless in domesticating your sexual drives, you will end up behaving worse than an animal. If you don't discipline your sexual needs, you may end up demanding sexual favors from any woman who happens to be closer to you, including your sisters, own mother, or even young babies. A man's sexual organ is brainless and small, but if not properly disciplined, controlled, and guided, it may overthrow one's brains. Never allow it to do the thinking for you. It's not its job. Now, if you allow a brainless organ to do the thinking for you, the results are devastating. It would lead you into the hell of your own making. Never allow it to do your thinking because it's mischievous and treacherous.

As you continue to interact with your peers, you will hear a lot of loose talk about their alleged sensual escapades. Don't be misled by such boy talk concerning hedonistic issues because most of that talk is mere fantasy. It emanates from one's imagination. When I was your age, I knew of many boys who would solemnly speak about the sacred lands that they had passionately treaded. They would preach about the sanctified pots in which they had cooked and devoured sacred meals. They would sermonize about the deepest and holiest wells from which they had quenched their seemingly insatiable carnal thirst. But I discovered one thing—most of what they said was a figment of their fertile venereal imaginations. Most boys lie about such things.

Don't run away from such boys because their stories are didactic in nature. Listen to their stories, lest you become outcasts, but don't take what they say as biblical truth. Don't try to put into practice what they claim to have accomplished sexually, because that can be the beginning of your undoing. This doesn't mean that you shouldn't learn from your peers. You should. But, take everything that they teach you with a pinch of salt. That's what an enlightened young man does.

Everything has its time, my sons, and if you wait patiently, the arrival of that time will never miss you. When you become of age, you will find women to love, and if they happen to be the right ones, then marry them. In your search for wives, don't look for angels because many men who spent most of their hay days hunting for angels ended up marrying devils. Don't be deceived by facial looks because they are as treacherous as quicksand. Never fall in love with a woman only because of her facial beauty because it fades away. Don't. My sons, look for character and a good heart because those virtues live in a female forever.

When men are still young, single, and searching, their ultimate dream is to marry an angelic and ideal woman. But, as men continue to grow in experience and wisdom, their idealism is repeatedly challenged by realism, and they usually forego the pursuit of angelic beauty, and begin to look for a woman who possesses a good heart. Of course, some few men are luckier than the rest because they find both angelic beauty and goodness of the heart in the woman they marry. There is no guarantee that you can be the luckier ones. Marriage is supposed to be a lifelong commitment, and can happily be spent with a good woman, though not quite good looking, than with a gorgeous woman who lacks a good heart.

My sons, love and protect your own and other people's children. Don't harm them in any way. Look at how some societies have imprisoned their children in their homes. Children can no longer play outside because it's no longer safe to do so. There is always some evil person hovering around, ready to snatch them away. For most kids, playing outside is like playing in hell. The ubiquitous human devil is prowling around looking for unprotected kids to devour. It's very sad indeed. That hell wasn't created by the kids themselves, but by adults. Don't touch people's kids unless they give you permission to do so. Don't even look at them admiringly because you may be misconstrued as a pedophile. I wonder what the society would have to do to bring freedom and safety to our kids again. To make our neighborhoods safe again so that our kids can be kids. As for you, make all kids around you feel safe.

My sons, please, love your wives and allow them to love you in return. Protect and make them feel safe. Respect them despite all their faults as human beings. Don't impose your trust upon them, but allow them to earn it. Earned credibility is difficult to take away, and it doesn't fade away easily. If you want your wives to believe you, you too should win their trust rather than demanding it in a silver platter. Don't abuse the confidence that you get from them. Never be afraid to relearn to trust, love, and confide. Take advantage of every opportunity to learn to trust again.

My sons, be faithful to your future spouses. Never, involve yourselves in extra marital affairs, or the so-called "small houses." They destroy your lives and families. Small houses force you to neglect your wife and children. You become a cheat. Small houses are like any other forbidden waters, they are sweet at first, but they make you lose your integrity, peace of mind, and respect, as a human being. They teach you to be dishonest to your wife and children. They create hatred between you and those members of your family who try to give you advice against them. Some may infect you with deadly, sexually transmitted diseases, such as HIV/AIDS. Don't allow other men to lie to you about how ladies taste differently because all waters taste the same. You must know that there is more to life than libidinous intimacy. Don't live for sex, but let sex spice up your life.

My sons, I want you to know that many young men worry about the size of their manhood. They fantasize of having a monster, robust, and sturdy manhood because they think that such a tool is more effective in pleasing their partner than a smaller one. I want you to know this fact: there are many natural things that a man can change, either for better or for worse, but no man can change the size of his manhood. Even those who have money, and try modern technology, sometimes end up with too big and ineffective a tool. The size of your tool is something that Mother Nature decided, and her wisdom can't be questioned. You should know that whatever the size of your machine is, you can't alter it no matter how much you worry about it. In fact, it's just a myth to think that the biggest male tool is the most efficient and fulfilling one. Experts in those matters say that what's significant in any gratifying sexual encounter is the amount of love, compassion, kindness, tenderness, grace, tolerance, and patience that accompanies the physical act, not the thickness or length of the tools that one uses. Just as you can't judge the efficacy of a farmer by the size of his farming equipment, but by the amount of his produce, likewise, sexual gratification isn't measured by the size of one's tools, but by the harvest produced by those tools.

Many women are unhappy in their marital bedrooms, not because their husbands are found wanting in terms of their male equipment endowment, but because their partners don't know how to use such equipment to the satisfaction of their spouses. You should accept what they say about dynamite—it comes in small packages. Most wars aren't won by the use of military tanks only, but by the use of small arms that are skillfully utilized. Whatever the caliber of your gun, use it efficiently like there is no tomorrow. The sexual encounter is like eating good food. Food's deliciousness is felt in the mouth, not in the stomach. If you want to savor the tastefulness of food, you should let it stay in the mouth a little bit longer. Those who are quick to swallow before they chew their food may end up doing a disservice to their bellies.

I am not an expert on self-gratification, my sons. Nobody ever claims to be. But one thing I know for sure is that, it's one of the most embarrassing and hardest issues to discuss, although it's a reality, and talking about it, is crucial to every young man. As you may know, some religious traditions teach that self-stimulation is harmful to one's spiritual and psychological growth. I don't contest that. Truly, it would foolhardy for me to contest their sentiments. However, I know for certain that, it's very natural. It's part and parcel of growing up, and you must know that most young people do practice it. If you want to do it, follow your conscience. If your conscience doesn't blame you, then you will be at peace with yourself. Just be discreet and clean. Self-gratification is one of those things that shouldn't be done in public. If other boys get to know that you indulge yourself, they might laugh at you. If you are ever caught with your pants down, here is the sign: he who laughs the wildest and loudest, practices it the most frequent.

But be careful. Self-satisfaction is addictive. You should remember to stop doing it once you get married, or even earlier, if you can. There is no need for a couple that lives together to indulge in such acts because that would show their selfishness. Of course, we can't compare weaknesses, but I feel that self-gratification is a better evil than engaging in premarital sex. Self-gratification does no harm to anybody, and if it does, the victim is the perpetrator. It neither passes diseases to anyone, nor does it impregnate anyone. It's a God-given gift to enable the not yet married to vent out their carnal compulsions in a non-destructive way.

My sons, you must also have self-control when it comes to food. Food is good for the body and was created to nourish it, but not the other way around. Control yourself when it comes to food, especially meat. You must always remember that meat tastes good to most people who eat it, and there are many times when one can't just have enough of it. Like any other food, meat must be shared. Most people like meat. Some people are greedy, when it comes to meat. The difference between those who like meat and the greedy is that the greedy can't control themselves when they see meat. In my wretched life, I have met greedy people who think that they should be entitled to all of it at the expense of fellow diners. Learn to share your food with others.

There is a fine line between liking meat and being greedy. Although meat is good, for both the body and the taste buds, it must be shared by those who eat together. When you have an opportunity to serve yourselves at the table, think of others. Fellow diners will judge if you are a gentleman by the quantity of meat that you pile on your plate. People like meat, but the only difference between greedy people and balanced people is that the greedy think that they like it more than others and therefore must be allowed to have the lion's share. Think of others. It's noble to walk out of the dining hall with a half-full stomach, than with a full stomach at the starvation of your fellow diners. Before you pile your plate with food, always check if your fellow guests need some more food. Learn to offer food to others, rather than being offered food all the time.

Don't be so picky when it comes to food. A fastidious guest is disgraceful to those who sit around the table with him. Eat what is placed on the table by your hosts unless you are allergic to it, or if it's poisonous. Don't forget to thank the cook even if you think that the food wasn't up to scratch. Remember that food tastes differently to different people. Your taste buds are not the only standard to measure the goodness of food. If you don't like the food, please, don't curse the cook. Curse your taste buds.

My sons, when you become of age, you will be allowed to drink alcoholic beverages, just like other adults do. I started drinking at the ripe age of thirty, and I knew exactly what I was getting myself into. I had figured out how I was going to control my drinking. Every country has laws that govern the consumption of alcoholic beverages, and such laws should be adhered to, strictly. If you happen to be one of those who cherish to partake in the drinking of those *sacred waters*, don't overdo it. Know your limits.

My sons, never drink and drive. Never drink and drive, I repeat. Some of the people who drink and drive end up getting involved in accidents. Of course, accidents happen even to sober people, and that's why they are called accidents. But, never allow people to think that your driving prowess was impaired by alcohol. Accidents take away innocent lives. Life is sacred, and should never be taken away by anyone. Human life is more precious than consuming a pint of beer. If you decide to drink, stay away from the steering wheel, and you will live longer and freely. If you want to stay away from prison, you should stay away from the steering wheel after drinking.

Drink responsibly, and never blame your behavior on alcohol. If you have a bone to chew with anybody, please, don't wait until you are drunk. Sober minds should undertake serious discussions. I know of many people who postpone serious discussions with members of their families with whom they have disagreements, until they are drunk. If you have anything to say to anyone, don't wait until you drink alcohol. Don't fight wars when you are drunk. Alcohol impairs your reasoning faculties. Don't insult people when you are drunk. If alcohol makes you pugnacious, please, don't consume it.

Average beer drinking doesn't impoverish anybody as some people might think. Yes, when one drinks alcoholic beverages, money is spent just like in any other pursuits of the bodily pleasures. Rome wasn't built by the people who drank non-alcoholic drinks alone. Never judge a man's intellectual ability by the amount of beer he drinks. If you decide to abstain from drinking alcoholic beverages, don't think that those who drink are foolish. Fools are found amongst both the drinkers and non-drinkers. At least, drinkers may blame their foolishness on alcohol, but the non-drinkers must shoulder the blame. They have no scapegoat.

However, you should know that alcohol is addictive. If it deters you from pursuing and achieving your goals and dreams, then you must stop consuming it. If beer prevents you from being the father or lover you should be, please, renounce it. If alcohol prevents you from making friends that you deserve, then forgo it. If beer prevents you from performing your work to the best of your abilities, please, discard it. If beer makes you sick, please stop taking it. If beer forces you to squander all your savings, then stay away from it. If alcohol prevents you from respecting other people, please, relinquish it.

Those in the know say that alcohol may affect your liver. The people who abuse it should be ready for the time of reckoning, when their health gives up on them. I have seen many people lying on those lonely hospital beds waiting, this time not for the next beer refill, but for an untimely heavenly call. I have heard some of them regretting about not taking good care of themselves, but some things can't be undone. My sons, take good care of yourselves so that you won't blame yourselves for your impending demise. It's hard enough to watch your death coming, harder to think that you are the cause of your own quietus, and hardest to imagine that it could have been prevented.

My sons, don't smoke tobacco (cigarettes). Please, never try smoking. I earnestly beseech you. I never tried it myself, and I don't regret it. Tobacco is highly addictive. Most of the people who got themselves into the smoking habit have enslaved themselves. Most of them realize quite late that they get nothing from smoking but nicotine, and in most cases, it would be too late to redeem themselves. Let me tell you this open secret about smoking. In some countries, smokers find themselves increasingly being isolated and ostracized by their families and communities. For instance, in most countries, smokers aren't allowed to smoke in most public places, and even in their own houses. Some companies have begun to shun smokers when they recruit employees. Don't start a battle that you will never be able to quit, even when you concede defeat. Don't get yourself into something that will enslave you for life, and make you a social misfit.

I don't intend to rule out the possibility of being able to stop smoking because some smokers successfully quit smoking. Sometimes, they manage to extricate themselves out of the habit through their own powers, and at other times, with the help of professionals and friends. Smoking is one of those things that look very neat and attractive when you are young because of peer pressure, but sooner or later you begin to see how unnecessary and unbeneficial it is. Unfortunately, at that time, the habit would be very difficult to break. So, my advice is that, if you don't want to fight unwinnable and unnecessary battles in the future, don't start smoking. If you don't wish to feel unwanted, disrespected, vulnerable, and ostracized in the future, please, don't start smoking.

But my sons, never segregate against smokers. Never think that they don't know what smoking does to their bodies and relationships—they do. They do care. Some try to stop smoking to no avail. Don't blame them. They need your support and kindness. They need your understanding and acceptance, not ostracization. They need understanding and healing. Don't tell them to stop because you aren't the first one to tell them that. Don't remind them that smoking kills because they have heard about it a thousand times. They need love and understanding. They need time. They need enough energy and motivation to quit.

My sons, anger is one of the feelings that all human beings experience in their lives. The only difference people have is that some people can control their anger, and others can't. Some people try to domesticate their anger, but others allow their anger to engulf them. My sons, you will experience both justified and unjustified anger in your lives. There is no question about it. You will meet people, things, events, and situations that will make you angry, but in all these nasty encounters, you have one big consolation—anger can be controlled and managed. Of course, you might not be able to control other people's anger, but at least, you can control yours. One of the biggest mistakes some people make is to think that they have a monopoly to anger and violence. They easily forget that everybody else can get angry too.

Although anger isn't an evil feeling, it must be managed appropriately. Learn to control your anger because if you don't, you will either end up in prison or in the grave. Anger shouldn't lead you to physical fighting with people because if you do that you may end up injuring or killing someone. Ordinarily, most people conquer provocative situations by fighting, rather than fleeing. However, history proves that there are many times when people overcome such situations by flight, rather than fighting. Those who run away from their enemies may live to see another day. But those who vow to die fighting may indeed die during the fight. If you are to fight, don't just choose your opponents, indiscriminately. Choose responsible adversaries, for they know when to flee if beaten, or when to stop beating the opponent, if victorious.

Of course, life will present you with situations where you have to fight. Fight. You will encounter situations where you have to defend yourself and those people you love through fighting. Do it. Fight to defend your rights and the rights of people who have been entrusted to your protection. Defend your children. Fight for your wife. Protect your family. Don't give your back to your friends in times of need. Defend your country, even with your own life. In such situations, fleeing is cowardice and treachery. Fight to defend and protect, and never be the aggressor. Never be the first to lay your hand upon your adversary except when trying to defend yourself.

Some fights are prevented through reasoning. Physical fighting should be relegated to the jungle, because brutes can't use their reasoning. People should resolve their problems and personal differences through dialogue. The ability to avoid fighting is a virtue of those men who can adequately and efficiently use their intellect. However, if you are to fight, fight to win. There is no wisdom in picking up a fight in which you will lose. If you think that you won't win a fight, resolve the contentious issues in non-violent ways. Don't embarrass yourself unnecessarily. It doesn't matter how angry you are, fighting should be the last resort.

My sons, it's good to be happy. I guess, human beings were created to be happy. However, happiness should be controlled too, because too much of it isn't good. You must always give yourself time for discernment amid your moments of merriment and joy. Yes, it's true that the purpose of life is the pursuit of happiness, but all pursuits of happiness shouldn't be absolute. Strike a balance.

When you are invited to a party, dance with those who are dancing, but always remember that others have their favorite dances and music as well. Give other dancers a chance to select their musical genres because they too give you that opportunity. After a while, you should withdraw to a corner and watch how others dance. It shouldn't be about your dance only, but other people's dances as well. Give yourself time to reflect and to learn new dances. A dancer who doesn't pause during the dance, and watch other dancers dancing, will neither acquire new dancing skills, nor improve his old ones.

When you are invited to a wedding, dance with those who are dancing, and eat with those who are eating, but give yourself moments of reflection. If you happen to amass lots of wealth, my sons, you have every reason to be happy, but don't forget that moments of reflection should be accommodated. You should also seek other people's happiness. It's not helpful to be the only happy person in a village of sorrowing people. There is no absolute happiness, my sons, because our happiness is tinged with sorrow. That's the nature of life. So, honorably, accept your moments of pain, and be thankful for every joyous moment you will encounter. Share the source of your happiness with others because the more, the merrier.

My sons, I don't know many things about drugs, but the little that I know I must emphasize. Never do drugs. Never try them. Drugs can ruin your lives. First, doing illegal drugs is a criminal offence in many countries. You may get away with it for a couple of times, but you should know that sooner or later you will be busted, and then sent to prison for many years. Once you get into jail, your chances of making it in life become slim. After your release, you may end up on the streets, and very much incapacitated by the drugs. Drugs can easily reduce your life to a perpetual hunt for them, and a never-ending marathon from the law enforcement agents.

Second, it's becoming more and more difficult for people who do drugs to get a job. Many employers send their prospective employees for drug testing, and once any traces of drugs are found in their bloodstream, then that's the end of it. No one wants to go to school for many years and then fail to get employment because of drugs. Doing drugs will ruin your chances of getting a job, and without a job you are nobody.

Third, drugs are addictive. Once you get into the habit of doing drugs, it may be very difficult for you to get out of the habit. Yes, there are some people who manage to extricate themselves from the habit, but many drug addicts fail to redeem themselves. Once the habit is formed, your whole lives will revolve around drug doing and dealing. I don't see the wisdom of getting into something from which one wouldn't be able to get out when one gets tired of doing it. Since it would be difficult for a drug addict to get a job or keep one, if employed, you would run short of money to buy more drugs, and that would push you into crime. If you don't get arrested for abusing drugs, you may be incarcerated for other crimes that are intimately associated with drug doing. Doing drugs makes your potential of being arrested more likely because they push you into the circles of like-minded friends, and those friends can push you into doing something that you never imagined doing.

Finally, some drugs are hazardous to health. Many times, we read about people who die because of drug overdose, either intentionally or unintentionally. My sons, you don't have to cut your lives short because of things that you can control. There are many diseases that are deadly in this world, and you shouldn't be a victim of something that you can prevent. If you do drugs, you end up suspecting everyone of hating you. You will end up being angry men. We didn't bring you over here to the U.S. to die prematurely. We came to the USA for a better future, and you don't get that from abusing drugs. There is no future in doing illegal drugs. In fact, drugs rob you of your dreams. They steal your family from you. They isolate you. They make you miserable.

My sons, never do drugs or even try them. It all starts with peer pressure, curiosity, and poor judgment, and then a habit develops. Once you get addicted, then you are in serious trouble, and you become a victim. The best therapy is to not get into drug doing. Many victims of drug abuse regret ever getting into that wretched habit. They find themselves alienated from themselves, their relatives, and the society. For many people who are addicted to drugs, the most frustrating challenge is that they can't just quit doing drugs because they have become unwilling slaves to the habit. My sons, if you want to win the war against drug addiction without incurring any losses, don't start abusing them. Drugs will never come knocking on your door, unless you invite them. Please, don't.

My sons, the creator, gave you wonderful skins to cover your bodies, and that was done once and for all. As free human beings, you have every right to do whatever you want with your skins. Some people have tattoos on their bodies, and I do respect their freedom to choose to have tattoos. I don't intend to take that right away from you, but there are certain things that you ought to consider before you decide to go for tattoos.

First of all, some tattoos are permanent. So, you need to think seriously about your tattooed future. You should remember that what looks nice today, may look ugly tomorrow. Think of how you would get rid of your permanent tattoos when you no longer like them. In addition, some tattoos have meanings that are tied to the context in which they were acquired. Before you opt for such tattoos, you need to research on whether their meaning will forever be the same. Remember, my sons, meanings and symbols are dynamic. What's believed to be a sacred and patriotic symbol today may be considered devilish in the future. Stay away from tattoos that will alienate you from others.

Furthermore, some professions have begun to shun people with visible tattoos due to the nature of the work they do. Are you going to choose to stay away from such professions because your body is visibly tattooed? Are you going to allow a tattoo to decide the type of jobs you will apply for? Getting a job is hard enough, don't limit your job opportunities because of a tattoo. Moreover, don't paint on your body an indelible tattoo of a lover or religious figure. Love, like everything else, lasts. What will you do when you fall out of love with someone whose tattoo you bear on your flesh? Likewise, religious allegiance changes.

Lastly, we are people with roots and a culture. Our culture has no room for tattoos. If you have indelible tattoos made on your body, it will be very difficult for you to fit well in our Zimbabwean culture. If you like art, let it be on paper, walls, or canvas, but not on your skin. Don't limit your relationships and job opportunities because of tattoos. I would encourage you to stop and think before you have tattoos on your bodies. Don't do anything to your body that you will regret in the future. The American dream is so evasive, delicate, and slippery that you shouldn't allow anything that you can avoid preventing you from achieving it. But don't despise the people that do have tattoos, for they know why they opted to have them. It's their choice, and it should be respected.

Although same-sex marriages have been legalized in some countries, they remain one of the most controversial issues in many cultures, families, and societies. This controversy could be a result of the human societies' lack of adequate understanding of the phenomenon. Also, it takes long for the society to change. More often than not, when humans don't have sufficient understanding of some social phenomenon, they may become suspicious of it. That suspicion may breed fear, which would eventually blossom into unwarranted hatred or even discrimination. But I say to you, never allow your lack of understanding of something or an issue to compel you to hate that which you don't quite understand.

We are Shona people of the Shumba Garwe totem. We belong to the *chidawo* (sub-totem), Sigauke. We now live in America. Although we are citizens in this country, you must remember that our citizenship is revocable. Yes, we have certain privileges, but we also have obligations. One of our privileges is that of practicing our culture freely, as long as it doesn't violate the Constitution of the United States. And it's good that we can still practice our own culture, and at the same time remain Americans. That's the beauty of America. One can maintain his cultural identity, yet remaining an American. You may eat your own food, drink your own drink, and wear your own clothes, but still remain American. But it's always noble to learn about other cultures. My sons, take advantage of every opportunity to learn the American culture, for it's your new home. But there are certain aspects of the home culture that don't just vanish. Cherish them. We are Americans, but that's not absolute. We are Shona, and that's absolute. That's our identity before we become Americans. As you know, circumstances beyond our own control may force us to go back to our country, Zimbabwe.

My sons, I want you to know that same sex unions are considered illegal in Zimbabwe, and perhaps, in other countries too. Same sex marriage isn't one of the cultural heritages of the Shona people, at least for now. Since culture is dynamic, we leave the door open for possible changes. Don't engage in a cultural practice that's deemed illegal by the country in which you were born. But always respect people whose culture is different from yours.

Our Shona culture doesn't allow persons of the same sex to have a conjugal relationship. Does that mean that there are no people with such attractions in Zimbabwe? No. We have them, and they were always there. However, they had to sacrifice their sexual orientation for the communal good. We belong to a collective culture, and we don't have any identity outside our community. I am, because we are, goes the philosophy of *unhu* (character) to which we subscribe. The Shona society prescribes that marriage be between persons of the opposite sex. The rationale behind that dictum being that every marriage must produce children, and for now, that's only possible in a heterosexual union. This worldview doesn't render different views invalid.

So, what's the way forward? My sons, although the American culture allows same sex unions and relationships, it also allows and supports heterosexual marriages and relationships. The American culture and Constitution provide you with what your Shona culture values—heterosexual marriages. Embrace that. Your right to marry women is guaranteed by the American Constitution. As a matter of fact, the American culture doesn't compel you to engage in cultural activities that aren't yours.

Be that as it may, you should respect people with different sexual orientations because they have the same rights as all other people. You should treat them with dignity because they too treat you with dignity. They too were created in the image of the Creator. You should never discriminate against them because they don't discriminate against you on account of your sexual orientation. Don't speak ill of them because they don't speak ill of you. Make friends among them, and benefit from their life experiences and lessons. Don't try to convert them to what you think is right, for they need respect, not conversion. Don't blame them for being who they are, for they need your love, not finger-pointing. They need your friendship, not your condemnation. Don't force them to see the reality the way you do.

My sons, it's your responsibility to defend and support the marginalized irrespective of their sexual orientation. Don't remain silent when they are being dehumanized and disfranchised. Don't do to them what you wouldn't want to be done to you.

My sons, discipline is the gateway to wisdom. Anyone who has self-control can achieve anything in life. Disciplining oneself is a life-long enterprise because new vices and temptations keep resurfacing. The fight is ongoing, but victory is certain for those who relentlessly fight. Be the master of your own body. Own and control it. Be the master of your own feelings. Own and control them. Blessed are those with self-control, for they shall be rewarded with peace, prosperity, longevity, good health, and freedom.

Political Involvement

Gudo guru peta mwise, vadoko vakutye (A leader should be humble in order to be respected by his/her followers).
Vushe madzoro, vunoravadzamwa (Kingship is rotational).

My sons, you might have heard that politics is a dirty game, but I don't think that it's all that dirty. In reality, it isn't a game at all, but a profession in which the richer and braver compete for public offices by attacking the integrity of their rivalries, sometimes using fabricated stories and issues. Occasionally, they campaign for support by promising certain developmental projects for the people. Politicians get their mandate to lead from other people. That mandate legitimatizes the political offices that they occupy, and the decisions that they make, supposedly on behalf of the people that they lead, and for the benefit of the society. Every democratic politician uses other people as ladders to ascend the political heights. There is no question about that. Many, after getting into office, may remove the ladder so that the people who would have voted them into power may have no access to them. You may not see your political representative until the next general elections.

In politics, if you aren't one of the politicians, you are left with no other option except to use your vote wisely to elect the politician by whom you would want to be governed. So, whether you accept to be represented or not, the elected politician's way of doing politics will affect you in one way or another. That's why it's imperative for every young person to be conscious of the politics of his home, village, country, and the world. Don't ever be politically illiterate, because that will count heavily against your country's welfare, and perhaps your children's future. Whether politics is a dirty or clean game, that doesn't matter, what matters is that you will be involved in politics whether you like it or not. You may choose to be either actively or passively involved, but either choice will affect you in one way or the other.

My sons, politics, start in the home and if not handled with care, can be very dangerous and destructive to your position as the head of your family. In home politics, your wife can be your political opponent. Usually, the contest concerns the love from children. Your kids' mother can discredit you among your children, and you will end up losing respect, dignity, and integrity in your own home. Some women can achieve that by constantly relating your mistakes to your children, in your absence, and by the time you come back home from work, all the children's eyes would be on you, to see if you are really the monster that their mother would have told them. Such women would give you a litany of some of the children's misdemeanors that would have happened when you weren't home so that you, as the father of the family, would discipline the culprits. The moment you try to discipline them, you give the children enough evidence that you are indeed the monster that their mother would have warned them about. Once your children begin to see you as such, then, no child would want to listen to your correction and advice. You will be the villain.

So, how does one neutralize such politics? Both parents should be involved in the disciplining of their children. Let the children know that both parents support each other when it comes to disciplinary matters. In fact, before implementing any disciplinary measures on children, parents should have a meeting so that they discuss the type and method of the disciplinary action they want to impose on the child. Discipline shouldn't be impromptu because that's likely to attract criticism from the mother of the children. Once that happens, children would hate the father. Do it together, or at least, agree to the form of punishment to be meted out to the kid.

My sons, it's both ways. Fathers too can turn their kids against their mother. Don't turn your children against their mother because kids are the only closest people she has in her marital home. She might be a bad person, but she remains the mother of her children, and therefore, sacred to them. Nobody can replace her in that position. Never criticize your wife in your children's presence because they would think that women should be criticized anywhere, any time. If you show respect to your wife in the presence of your kids, they will always respect their mother, and will do the same to their wives. Respect shown to a wife by her husband in the presence of their children will always inspire them to do the same to their wives. For most children, the only school that they learn about appropriate behavior in relationships is their home. You don't want to be a bad example to your children because that will count heavily against you and them.

My sons, probably one day you will want to be involved in larger politics of your country, and I would like you to know that there is nothing wrong with that. There are three ways in which you can get involved in politics at the national level. First, you may be involved in politics at an indifferent level. This indifference may be a result of your lack of interest in politics, or of political apathy. Some people who are in this level claim that they don't want to get involved in politics because it's a dirty game, and therefore, dangerous. Others claim that their voices don't make a difference because no one cares. Such people may refuse to partake in programs of national interests such as voting for their country's leaders and attending political rallies. Some of them may not want to talk, read, and even comment on politics. The people who belong to this category have decided not to know the politics around them because they want to stay indifferent.

My sons, if you decide to participate in politics in this way, you will make yourself miserable. Remember, politics is about the distribution of power, wealth, opportunities, and so on, among the citizens of a particular country. If you choose to be indifferent as far as politics is concerned, other people will select a destiny for you. They will choose leaders for you whether you like the leaders or not. If they choose good leaders, you will benefit just like the politically active citizens, but if an evil leader ascends the throne, you will be affected just as those people who would have taken a part in the election of that leader. Yes, you can choose to be indifferent in electing a political leader, but you won't have the option to be indifferent to the elected leader's misrule. You may stay in the comfort of your home and refuse to cast your vote for the leader of your country, but if an incompetent leader gets the job, you will be forced out of the comfort of your home, in search of greener pastures elsewhere.

My sons, if you choose not to cast your vote for a country's leader, and then an incompetent leader ascends the throne, your country's economy will suffer, and that has adverse effects upon you and the next generations. Bad leaders may enact evil laws that may end up affecting you directly or indirectly, as an individual and a member of your community. Never allow other people to determine your destiny when you can do so yourself. Bad leaders get democratic offices and power because good citizens have withdrawn from active politics. My sons, be actively involved in your country's politics and never be indifferent. As a citizen of your country, you have the obligation to elect leaders of your country, and you can ignore that responsibility at your own peril.

You might ask me, "Father, what do I do if I don't like all the fielded political candidates?" Of course, that situation is possible, but whenever you are asked to choose between two devils, my sons, please, elect the lesser evil, because you stand to suffer more if the worse devil becomes the leader. I know that there are times when it becomes so difficult to count the merits a political candidate has over the other, because most of them lie, but it's better to be lied to by a convincing liar than by an unbelievable one. In such cases, please trust your judgment. Never be indifferent. Those who choose apathy and indifference will forever be governed by fools or the people they don't like.

The second level at which you may get involved in politics is by becoming an active participant. Register to vote as soon as the opportunity is granted you. On the Election Day, be among the earliest to cast your vote. But don't just vote blindly. Your choice of a political candidate should be informed by reason. Listen to political debates by the candidates who belong to different political parties. If you live in a country where such discussions are forbidden, then get the information from the media. Don't vote for a politician just because of his good looks because beauty doesn't run a country. Don't cast your vote for a candidate just because he is young, for youthfulness and wisdom sometimes don't walk hand in glove. Don't go for an older man just because of his age, because stupidity isn't a monopoly of the inexperienced and young.

Run away from tribalism or regionalism because that's one of the greatest enemies of sound judgment in choosing a good leader. The fact that the candidate is related to you, or comes from the same region as you do, doesn't bring food to your table. Your vote shouldn't be predicted by the State or Province where you live, but it should go to the highest bidder. Any political leader who needs your vote should sweat for it. Many people who practice tribalism or regionalism in politics end up being used by political candidates. If I am one of the political candidates vying for a public office, and I am assured of your vote just because we come from the same area, or I have the same skin color as yours, then I wouldn't sweat to get your vote because it's already in my pocket. My sons, elect a person who you judge to have the capability to perform the work that must be done for the transformation of your community.

My sons, in most countries, leaders have terms in which they are allowed to rule their countries. Most States recommend two terms of about five years each. This upper limit is prescribed to allow leaders to give way to other people who might have new ideas of how to revamp the political and economic fortunes of their countries. Never stick by one candidate for too long because political leaders' wisdom, just like a water spring, runs dry. You must know that power is sweet, and because of that some leaders won't leave office willingly. If that happens in your country, then use your vote to get rid of such leaders. Don't be rigid in the way you do your politics, my sons. Please, allow some flexibility in your choice of leaders. Beware of Party politics because they may enslave you. Think outside your political Party. Some voters deprive themselves of good leaders just because good candidates don't belong to their political Parties.

Never allow any politician to force you to do immoral things so that he acquires or stays in power. Never accept any reward for harassing your candidate's political opponents. Don't allow your children to be used by politicians to harass the people who have different political perspectives. Unless the politician is your parent, you must know that there is no politician worth dying for. You also should know that politicians have a short memory. They tend to forget all the sacrifices their supporters make for them as soon as they occupy their public offices. I know of people who sacrificed their time, wealth, families, or even their very lives, who were never recognized or rewarded by the politicians that they supported.

Although your vote should be earned by any aspiring political candidate, it should never be up for sale. Selling a vote to the highest bidder is like selling one's heart and conscience to the devil. By selling your vote, you are surrendering the future of your country into the hands of an incapable man. Let those politicians who want to give you something just before the election, do that, but your conscience should lead you when you elect your country's leaders. I know of voters who have sold away their consciences, and the future of their countries by receiving a packet of sugar or a pint of beer from some incompetent politicians.

My sons, at this point, your question might be, "So, what do I do if a politician offers me something for my vote?" My honest answer is; accept the gift, but think of the country as a whole, and vote for a candidate who can do the job. In fact, there is no presidential candidate who walks around with a bag of money telling people that he or she is looking for votes to buy, but the money or other goodies are given away as gifts. So, accept the gifts as such but never allow them to influence your choice of the country's leaders. In fact, most competent leaders don't offer money in exchange for votes, but they offer economic development to their countries before and after they get into offices. You may get a meal from the sale of your vote to a politician, but you will deprive the next generation of a thousand meals. Don't hesitate to cast your vote because it's your right to do so. But do it wisely.

Don't be afraid to change your political opinion or party. You aren't a slave to your political opinions. No political party should own you. Blind political allegiance and affiliation impair one's political judgement, and may result in economic misery. Don't be a slave of any political party. Dangle your vote in the air so that the most capable person gets it. If there were no political Parties, public servants would work harder to earn the voters' trust. Because many people are blinded by political affiliation, some politicians rely on the name of the party, to be elected into office. He, who wants to have your vote, should earn it. Of course, a political candidate may fool you once, but don't allow anybody to deceive you twice.

The third level of political involvement you might want to pursue is becoming a politician yourself. If you decide to do that, don't allow politics to erode your moral fibers. Of course, it's part of the job description of a politician to make promises, at times, unrealistic ones, but don't make promises that you aren't willing to fulfill. I know of politicians who have promised the electorate that once they get into power, they would build bridges although there were no rivers in the area where the voters lived. Some politicians did promise the electorate a million jobs, but as soon as they got into offices, they formulated laws that would discourage any foreign investment in the country, and by so doing driving away potential investors. Some leaders promised their people housing for all, but as soon as they got into power, they authorized the destruction of the houses in which those people were living. My sons, don't promise anything that you wouldn't be willing to deliver. Don't make irrelevant and unachievable promises. Advise the electorate of the possibilities and challenges that lie ahead. The truth will set you free.

Never employ thugs to force people to vote for you. Never force fear down the throats of the electorate so that they may elect you even if they no longer like you. You should remember that those who come into political offices because of voters' fears will live to be afraid during and after their political terms. Furthermore, people can't be afraid forever. There always comes a time when the electorate gets exorcized of its demons of fear, and turn against you. If you want people to vote for you, please talk to them; convince them that what you would offer them once you get into office is superior to what your opponents can offer.

As you embark on your campaigns, you must know that those who live in glass houses shouldn't throw stones. Once you declare your interest in running for a public office, people are going to scrutinize your past, present, and future. If you have any plans of running for public office, you should lead a life that won't tarnish your reputation. You should have discipline in terms of sexual morality. Those who don't control themselves in terms of carnal passions will live to be sad. In the political profession, what you do in the utmost secrecy of your bedrooms will be paraded publicly in daylight. Your political opponents will use your moral disposition to destroy your political ambitions. Don't ever be found wanting in that respect. Your political office comes with a procession of interested women, but if you lose your head by allowing your male organ to do the thinking for you, those women can be the cause of your undoing. I know of leaders who almost lost everything that they had toiled for because of their failure to control their sexual drives.

I will be jubilant if the people vote for you to become one of their leaders. As soon as you ascend the throne you must know that the next thing in line is to descend from that throne. No one should want to rule forever because that's selfish. If you have anything to do for the country and for the people who elected you, the right time to do that is as soon as you get into office. Don't wait until the end of your term so that you can use those unfinished businesses as a reason for your perpetual occupancy of the political office. My sons, good leaders get elected, rule, and exit. There is nothing as nauseating as a leader who gets elected into public office, but then refuses to retire, even if he has nothing else to offer. Good leaders beget better leaders.

My sons, as a leader, you shouldn't always think of the next general election, but about the next generation. Make policies that benefit all the people, including the next generations. To get into politics for self-aggrandizement is a pernicious political crime. Never use people as means to your political achievements, but see all of them as ends in themselves.

You can't always win elections. Sooner or later you would be defeated, and you should accept that loss graciously. Wise losers congratulate their victorious opponents. Remember that your political opponents aren't your enemies; they are competitors. Never seek to harm them. Don't disrespect them. If you do something that attracts public scorn, please do apologize, and if need be, resign. People have more respect for leaders who try, fail, and then apologize, than the dishonest politicians who don't have the word "sorry" in their vocabulary.

Never teach your followers to hate supporters of your political adversary. Hatred isn't good for unity. It fans up economic instability. It consumes everyone. The same hate language that you encourage them to use for your opponent, will also be used against you in the future. Respect is the mark of great politicians.

As a leader, if you are to choose an economic ideology for your country, please, don't opt for communism. The mysteries of that political ideology don't cease to astonish me. Everything belongs to the people, yet some of those people aren't satisfied. Although some people aren't satisfied, they all vote for the Party. In communist countries, all people are equal, yet some people are more equal than others.

My sons, choose democracy. Yes, it has its evils, but it isn't as hypocritical as communism. Although democracy is the dictatorship of the majority over the minority, it's better to be dictated to by the majority than by a few top leaders who pretend to do it for all the people. Even if the democratically elected leaders were to dictate to you, at least, you show your disapproval of their rule by casting your vote for someone else. Yes, I know of some democratically elected leaders who have been accused of rigging elections, but I think that it's better to be ruled by an election rigger than by someone who hasn't even sweated to rig elections.

Like any other political ideologies, democracy has its own shortcomings. It's not every participating candidate who wins in a democratic plebiscite. Remember, it's the candidate who gets the majority votes who becomes the leader. And that leader might not be the one you support. What do you do when democracy gives you lemons? Crying every day until the next election? Make lemonade. Support the new leader in every possible way for the benefit of the country. Don't sabotage his initiatives. Avoid bitterness and anger. Congratulate the victor, and rejoice with his or her supporters. If you do that, they will also rejoice with you when your candidate wins.

My sons, don't allow politics to turn your friends into enemies. Don't run away from good fiends because they see politics through different lenses. After all, when the elections are over, what we remain with are our friends and relatives. Politicians become unapproachable, until the next election. Don't impose your political views on everyone else. People see things differently. If you have an opinion about politics, profess it with respect. Don't try to impose it on other people. If other people don't want to support your candidate, it doesn't mean that they are fools, but that they are different from you. You can't make everyone be like you.

In politics, you will always come to the point where people stop appreciating your contribution as their leader, please don't lose your head.

Never force them to like you. Don't hate them for their change of political allegiance. In fact, you should thank them for the opportunity that they would have offered you in the first place. The people owe you nothing, but you owe them your office and popularity. Don't use the same position to destroy their freedoms, aspirations, and dreams. If you are still convinced that you should occupy the office; talk to them; persuade them, and convince them. Don't force them. Any political loyalty born out of force will affect you heavily when you finally lose that office.

As a leader, you must shun corruption. There is nothing that destroys the political future of an individual, and a country's economy, more than corruption. Never associate with corrupt officials. Anybody who is accused of being corrupt must be investigated, and if found wanting, must be punished. In politics, you will have friends, but don't protect them if they become corrupt. Allow them to pay dearly for their nefarious activities. My sons, corruption is a cancerous and infectious problem that is very difficult to get rid of once it gets into the bloodstream of the people. Prevention is better than cure.

Always defend your people's rights. You must remember that even your political opponents do have human rights that need to be protected by you as their leader. People will say nasty things about you, but you must defend their freedom to speak. If you take to the habit of silencing your opponents, you will deprive yourself of an authentic source of feedback from which all successful leaders benefit. Your political adversaries make you a better person by pointing out the shortcomings that your friends might not be able to see. If you surround yourself with people who say what you want to hear, then you will never understand the other side of the story. Most of your friends will always try to convince you that the coin has one side, which all of us know is untrue. A leader who doesn't want to be criticized is like a soccer team that wish to play a soccer game without a referee.

As a leader, you mustn't pursue the policy of survival of the fittest because it's a very dangerous strategy to adopt for any country. If you adopt that policy, you will cause more suffering to many hardworking people who are just less fortunate. Survival of the fittest is a criminal policy that turns citizens against other citizens. As a leader, always have a special place in your heart for the less privileged members of your society. The poor must find a protector in their leader, not a destroyer. Protect them from harsh economic policies and exploitation by the rich. Uplift them. Create policies that allow them to realize their dreams. Don't buy into the irrational belief that claims that most people are poor because they are lazy. If hard work could transform somebody into a millionaire, then almost everyone would be one. It boggles my mind that some employers are billionaires, yet the people who work for them struggle to make ends meet.

My sons, in many countries, including Zimbabwe, demonstrations are legal and constitutional. They are a communication method that ordinary citizens of a particular country can use to alert their leaders of their grievances. Demonstrations can also bring such grievances to the attention of the international community and human rights watchdogs. Even though demonstrations are constitutional in Zimbabwe, they are supposed to be conducted in a peaceful manner. Disgruntled citizens have the right to express themselves by demonstrating provided they don't infringe on other people's rights.

Although demonstrations are legal in Zimbabwe, provided they follow the constitutional guidelines, they can turn violent. There are factors that can turn a peaceful demonstration to chaos. First, criminals and hooligans may take advantage of the large number of people on the streets, and may loot shops. These hooligans may not even know why people are demonstrating. The large numbers of people on the streets gives them a hide out.

Second, political opportunists may incite a few of their members to employ violence in order to push a political agenda. It takes only one person throwing a stone at a car or shop windows for violence to erupt. Third, politicians can implant trouble makers in the demonstrating group to give a negative portrayal of the demonstrators. These planted trouble makers can deliberately instigate violence. My sons, human beings can organize peaceful demonstrations, but there is always the likelihood of a demonstration turning nasty.

If the demonstrations turn violent, the government has no other choice except to deploy police officers, mainly the riot police. In most countries, police officers have two primary responsibilities—protecting personal and public property and preserving life. During a riot, it's their constitutional duty to protect property from wanton destruction, and to preserve life of the rioters and those people that might be caught in the crossfire. It's their job. They have a code of ethics just like all other professionals. But, my sons, don't ever forget that they too have weaknesses and fears just like all of us. Although we expect them to be ethical, they can be corrupt and unprofessional. Although we expect them to be stoic and forgiving, they may give way to anger and the need to retaliate against demonstrators. Yes, they sometimes make errors of judgment.

Whatever you do in such a demonstration, don't fight the police because they aren't your enemies. If you decide to fight them, you won't win. Don't ever start a war that you can't win. You don't win a battle against the police because they are armed with the law. They have baton sticks, shields, handcuffs, helmets, and at times, firearms. Don't give them a reason to beat you up. Don't give them a reason to arrest you. Just go back home, my sons. Fighting police officers is a battle you won't win. So, don't do it. It doesn't matter how noble your cause is, don't fight the police.

If you manage to beat up the police, that's not the end of the story. The government can't just fold its hands and allow the rioters to wreak havoc. It sends in the army. When things come to that stage, run for your life, my sons. Soldiers aren't police officers. They don't have teargas. They don't have riot helmets. They don't have handcuffs. They don't have baton sticks. They do have lethal weapons—guns. Sometimes, they don't even have rubber bullets, but live ones. Their intervention is deadly.

My sons, don't destroy private or public property during demonstrations. Other people do have their constitutional rights to own property just like you. It's a criminal act to destroy other people's property. Don't destroy public property because it belongs to every Zimbabwean. It's funded by public funds that are mainly generated from the taxes that everyone pays. If you vandalize police cars, they shall be replaced in the future, and you will pay for their replacement. Instead of purchasing ambulances or books for school children, the tax money is diverted to replace the police vehicles because we need them. If you destroy public property, you are vandalizing your own property, and you will pay for it in one way or another.

My sons, law enforcement agents may seem unnecessary in times of demonstrations, but there always comes a time when you need their service. Follow their constitutional commands. Respect them because they are on your side. Know your limits, and the things you can possibly achieve without endangering your own lives or other people's.

My sons, refuse to be manipulated by politicians or the mob. The mob doesn't think. Don't surrender your principles in exchange for being accepted by your peers or political leaders. Don't be coerced into doing something that's not right. Always use your conscience. Don't loot during demonstrations because that's stealing. Don't incite others to loot.

Always remember that there are consequences to your actions. Some of the consequences may look disproportionate to your misdemeanors, but that's what the law does. At most times, when the time of reckoning arrives, you are likely to face the consequences alone. Usually, the perpetrators of criminal activities run away. In chaotic demonstrations and battles against law enforcement agents, innocent people—the bystanders may be caught in the crossfire. Don't allow your actions to cause unnecessary suffering for innocent people.

After all is said, it doesn't matter whether politics is a clean or dirty game, it should be played responsibly. You should get involved, and never allow other human beings to decide your destiny for you. Cast your vote when the time to do so comes. Never give in to voter apathy because it allows bad politicians to lead. Voter apathy breeds dictatorship and oppression. If you become a leader, rule responsibly and accountably. Don't endeavor to rule forever, for there is a limit to what a leader can achieve. Don't forget to pass on the leadership baton to other citizens because you weren't created alone. God gave you brothers and sisters, equally capable, or even more capable than you. Leaders become who they are because other leaders pass on the leadership office to them. Never deprive other citizens of the opportunity to lead.

My sons, be concerned with the politics of your country. Don't be afraid of politics. Those who fear to get involved in the politics of their land shall live to be governed by fools. In democratic politics, no one is powerless. Your vote is your power. Don't give it for free. Let the winning candidate earn it. Use it to influence the way your country is governed. If you happen to be the politician, convince the voters that you are worthy of their votes. I agree that politics may be a dirty game, not only to the politicians, but also to the governed. It's better to get dirty as a player than a spectator. My sons, be politically aware, active, and decisive. Some countries are run by fools and despots because their supporters lack political awareness, action, wisdom, and decisiveness.

Friendship

Rume rimwe harikombi churu (Unity enables people to achieve their goals). *Varara vese havanyimani magaro* (The people who associate with each other will soon share a common behavioral trait).

My sons, it's good that human beings get involved in friendship. Friends do come in different colors and shapes. In your entire lives, you will meet and make a myriad of friends. Friends play a significant role in one's life. You need them, and they need you too. Some friends come and go, but you will always have some who linger around longer. Some stay for life, and others for a moment, but all are friends. Friendship is something that shouldn't be resisted. One thing to remember is that some friends are good, and others are bad. You should avoid bad friends at all costs.

Good friends can be identified by their characteristics. They are trustworthy. You can share your secrets with them, and they will never spread them maliciously. You can entrust them with your precious property, such as a car, and they will never wreck it. If anything happens to your property that is temporarily under a good friend's jurisdiction, a good friend would help you fix it. You can loan them some money, and they will return it in good time. You can entrust them with the safety and protection of your family, and they will sacrifice their lives for them. You can share your weaknesses and vulnerabilities with them, and they will never use them against you, or share them with anyone else, or even run away from you because of them. You can disclose your wildest dreams and decisions to them, and they will never laugh at you.

Good friends don't run away from you when you suffer the consequences of your wrong decisions. You can dream aloud in their presence, and they will never undermine your capabilities to pursue and achieve those dreams. You may reveal your shameful secrets to them, and they will never sing about them from hilltops. Good friends give you advice, while also respecting your judgments, choices, and decisions. They also confide in you because you honor their secrets.

Good friends are a source of strength and comfort during times of need. They stand by you through thick and thin, when other people betray you. They may accompany you through the valley of the shadow of death, and never expect compensation in return. When no one else can give you the support that you need, a good friend is all you need. They rejoice with you when you rejoice, and they mourn with you during your time of grieving. They celebrate your success as if it were theirs, and they empathize with you when you encounter challenges.

Good friends force you to surpass your imagined limits by encouraging you to try again. They inspire you to do your best to achieve your goals. They also assist you to conquer the demons of fear. Fear of failure is the greatest impediment to innovation. There are many things that we should have achieved, but we didn't, just because no one gave us the encouragement and assurance that we needed. A single word of encouragement from a friend makes you want to do better and achieve more.

My sons, you will meet people who will flatter you, but real friends will tell you the truth that will mold you into better persons. They give you advice, but they don't impose it upon you. They let you be yourself. They love you despite all your imperfections. They sacrifice their comfort for your sake. They respect you for what you are: a human being. When they have their problems, they share them with you. If you find such a friend, do treasure him or her.

My sons, don't forget to give your friends good advice and friendly correction if necessary. You should remember that good advice is never offered as the only option a friend has, but as one of the many possibilities that your friend may want to explore further. Any piece of advice, however noble, may seem intrusive, if imposed upon a friend.

If a good friend wrongs you, please, don't hesitate to inform him. If he genuinely asks for forgiveness, please, do offer it. If you wrong a friend, go and ask for forgiveness. To say, "I am sorry," is a sign of a disciplined person. Many battles are fought not because people don't have anything else to do, but because some people don't have the humility to apologize. A friend who thinks that he is always right may mislead you. Such a friend might try to live your life for you, which is a very sad thing. Take advice from friends, but make it your prerogative to make your own decisions. Don't blame your advisors for the decisions that you make because it's your responsibility to use their advice, or to respectfully discard it.

You should remember that friendship is sometimes dynamic. Like most things in life, friendship does expire, but that shouldn't bother you. In life, you will continue to meet and make new friends, take advantage of that. When old friends leave you, don't be afraid to move on with life. But, never forget the old friends. You should also allow your former friends to make new friends, because that's how friendship goes. Don't monopolize on friendship because what you see in your friends is what other people see in them as well. Don't stick with an old friend if he wants to move on with new friends. It doesn't mean that you are a bad person when your friends leave you, for it might be a sign that you are too good for them. But never abandon an old friend who needs your help. Always hasten to help old friends for the good old golden days.

When a friend gets married, don't forget that his wife becomes his closest friend. Allow your old friend to have quality time with his spouse. Don't interfere with their affair. Don't judge his wife. Don't support your friend, if he is abusive to his wife. Don't encourage a friend to cheat on his wife because you don't want your wife's friend to do the same to your wife. Don't ever criticize your friend's wife even if she deserves such criticism because she isn't your wife. If your friend's spouse doesn't like you, it might be the right time to part ways with your friend because his allegiance should be to his wife, first and foremost.

Your friend's wife isn't necessarily your friend. Don't impose yourself upon her. Don't backstab your friend with his wife because you don't want your friends to do the same about you. Don't discuss your friend's past and present weaknesses with his wife, for it's unforgivable. Whatever you do, don't fall in love with your friend's wife because that's the surest way of breeding murderous animosity with your friend. Your friend's children aren't your kids, so treat them with respect. Don't take advantage of their trust on you to prey on them. His daughters may be gorgeous, but their beauty isn't for your shameful carnal escapades. A good friend may forgive you for a thousand wrongs, but not for desecrating and violating his wife or daughters.

You will meet many bad friends, and you will recognize them by their colors. They befriend you because they want something from you. When they get what they wanted, they immediately leave you. They abandon you when you most need them because they were never your friends in the first place. Such friends become jealous of your success. If you share your worries and problems with them, they shout them from the hilltops. They may give you bad advice so that you don't succeed in life. When they are with you, they pretend to empathize with you, but laugh at you when you are gone. They promise to take care of your family when you are away, yet they are busy desecrating your wife or daughters.

They expect favors from you without thinking of reciprocating them. Some of them can't even say, "Thank you." They beg you for favors, and once they get what they want from you, you don't see them again until they want something from you again. If you tell them any secrets of yours, they share them with your enemies. When you get into trouble, they run away from you, and clandestinely celebrate your downfall. When you fall, they secretly celebrate your disgrace.

They praise you for your wisdom when present, but preach about your foolishness in your absence. They invite you to their homes, but they perfume their houses when you are gone because they think that you stink. They buy you alcoholic drinks like there is no tomorrow, but despise you when you get drunk. They help you date a woman of loose morale, but secretly laugh at you for marrying a prostitute. They offer you food when you are hungry, but they complain to the public that you are a basket case.

When you are with them, they pretend to laugh with you, but when you are gone, they laugh at you. They praise you when you are present, but they insult you when you are absent. They pretend to smile at you, when, in fact, they are frowning at you. They pretend to cheer you up, when in fact, they are jeering you down. They may encourage you to think, yet they may try to control your life by doing all your thinking. Either you take their advice, or they consider you stupid.

My sons, you must remember that your first responsibility is towards your family, and you should always give priority to it, but that doesn't prohibit you from making sacrifices for your friends. Don't hesitate to abandon evil friends because if you don't, you would end up in jail. It's better to stay alone, than in the company of bad friends.

Facebook is one of the greatest social media achievements of our generation. I have been on Facebook for several years now, and I have had the opportunity to learn about my friends' personalities and characteristics by observing their postings or lack of. The following are the types that I came up with:

Hero worshipers are the sycophants who are always ready to praise a friend's comments without critically analyzing them. They flatter their hero most of the time. They compete to praise the hero more often than not. It's true that sometimes people agree with each other's views, but when that happens all the time, then, something is wrong. These friends sometimes create heroes. Their comments are always positive.

However, their main problem is that they don't critically examine their hero's posts thereby depriving him or her of the growth that comes from constructive criticism. They avoid negative criticism of the hero because they don't want to be unfriended. They can get angry on behalf of their hero. In fact, some of the Facebook heroes, from time to time, compel their friends to agree with them by threatening to unfriend them, if they dare criticize them. My sons, don't become Facebook hero worshipers or bootlickers, for it's disgustful. Always speak your mind, even if that leads to the end of your friendship with someone.

Likers are lazy friends who have no time to type comments. They can't resist the temptation to click the "like" option, in whatever situation. They "like" whatever is posted; be it death, sadness, happiness, pictures, wisdom, or stupidity. At the end of the day, one wonders what these people mean by "like" because I don't see anything to like about death. Likers are nice people because they are primarily positive. However, there are times when it becomes difficult to tell why they like what they say they like. My sons, spare a moment and write something in response to your friend's postings. Don't just "like" postings without writing a comment. Your "likes" should be sensible.

The "I-know-it-all" facebookers are more concerned about their comments than what their friends share. They bombard their friends with wise but impractical sayings. They don't have time to read, reflect, and comment on other people's posts. They don't believe that they can learn anything from anybody else. They are proud and overconfident people. Their pride prevents them from appreciating and analyzing other people's postings. If anyone constructively criticizes them, they quickly delete that comment, or they unceremoniously unfriend that friend. They don't like a give and take situation because they should be the givers, all the time. My sons, it doesn't matter how uneducated your friends might be; treat them as equals. If you want them to appreciate what you write, you too, should appreciate what they write. Please, stay away from unappreciative friends because they use you to boost their egos.

Well-wishers are the friends who wish others good mornings and good nights whenever they wake up or go to bed, respectively. They aren't interested in any other thing except wishing others good tidings. They firmly believe that their wishes can make a difference in other people's lives. They don't participate in debates that take place in the social forum between their "good mornings" and "good nights." They are good people because they herald the coming of a new day and a new evening. Their primary problem is that they don't realize that their friends need more than just glad tidings.

Mourners post something on Facebook whenever they encounter a challenge in life. Usually, they just write a short statement expressing their sadness or anger. When friends ask them to elaborate on their situation, they then ask the enquirer to inbox them. One good thing about them is that, they refuse to suffer in silence. They want the whole world to suffer with them. However, their primary problem is that they share their sorrow, but refuse to give the details about its causes. They never realize how disturbing some of their posts are to people who don't know the whole story. Don't ever be one of them. Never share your tribulations on Facebook unless you are ready to give details about them.

Family worshippers venerate their lovers, children, and parents. They post every picture of their beloved ones. Sometimes, they put up their beloved ones' photos as their profile pictures. Some of them post their pastors' photos as their profile pictures. The best thing about these guys is that they appreciate their family members. However, sometimes this appreciation becomes too exaggerated. Your Facebook friends want to see your own pictures, not your pastor's picture because they can view the pastor' photos on his Facebook page. Be yourself.

Low self-esteem people are those who don't trust and appreciate what and who they are. They use other people's pictures as their profile pictures. They lie about their ages, academic background, and occupations. They try to hide their true selves from the public. They present a false picture of themselves to their Facebook friends. However, the lies they tell about themselves help boost their self-esteem. But, my sons, be what you are. You might like Nelson Mandela, but you aren't him. You might like Barack Obama, but there is only one Barack Obama, and that's not you. Create your own name and legacy. Don't deprive Obama's kids of their father's profile pictures. Be inspired by celebrities, but be yourselves.

Sanctimoniacs are also known as Facebook preachers. They post good biblical passages, Christian hymns, prayers, pictures, and sayings. They have no time to comment on other people's postings. They believe that their mission on Facebook is to preach, give testimonies, and convert others. Their postings bless some readers, but many don't read them. Their main problem is that they think they can save evildoers on Facebook. Your faith is good for you, and you should keep it to yourself. Don't send Facebook friends chain prayers or Novenas so that you may receive blessings because God doesn't operate that way. People come to Facebook for friends, not for conversion. They know where to go to find religion.

Politicians' primary concern on Facebook is to recruit political adherents by advertising their political ideologies. They know that in politics one has to merit the support he or she gets, so, they advertise themselves. Their primary problem is that they criticize other politicians yet can't stomach any criticism themselves however constructive it is. Most of them want to surround themselves with people who always agree with what they post. If you don't praise them, they unfriend you. My sons, never mistake your Facebook friends for political dunderheads because they are wise people. If you want them to be your political followers, invite them to your rally.

Soccer people praise their teams when they are doing okay, but mourn bitterly, when their teams aren't performing well. They worship their soccer teams and try to recruit more fans for their teams. They claim to know more about soccer than the soccer coaches. They praise some soccer players, but chastise others. Sometimes they shout at, and curse those people who don't support their teams. Some of them know more about soccer players than they do about their family members.

One significant challenge that bedevils these people is egoism, especially when their teams win. They use boastful language to describe their exploits. Some of them are very loyal to their soccer teams. They keep supporting them, even when they aren't doing well. My sons, respect other people's teams. Don't create enemies because of soccer. When you celebrate your team's victory today, never forget that the same team will be the underdog of tomorrow.

The picture people post pictures only. They appreciate their beauty or lack of it. They want to impress their friends by posting pictures of their unsuspecting friends and celebrities, sometimes embracing them. If they are men, they post pictures in which they are in the company of beautiful ladies, cars, buildings, and while eating delicious food. Their major challenge is that of pomposity. Sometimes they post other people's pictures without being given express permission to do so. However, they are friendly people who appreciate God's blessings.

Story-tellers post stories that they have written themselves or stories that they have read somewhere. They usually post very entertaining stories. They are entertainers. Some of their stories make splendid reading, but others are just not so good. Sometimes they can't resist the temptation to copy and paste stories. This copying and pasting discourages them from being original in their story-telling. Although it's easier to retell stories that you have heard elsewhere, it's always noble to compose your own stories. No one becomes a seasoned story-teller by only narrating other people's stories—write your own stories. Be original.

The titters are also called, the "kikikiki" or "LOL" people. They sometimes don't write any comments, they just laugh. They don't hide their laughter. They are excellent people because they laugh at almost everything. However, sometimes they write nothing except "LOL" which might not help their friends. In the traditional rural setting, they are fit for "skinning goats" whilst others are talking serious business. If you want people to take you seriously on social media, don't just laugh; say something.

Sojourners want all their friends to know that they have gone to visit some places. They share the progression of their journeys on Facebook. The good thing about these friends is that you know where they go and when they come back. Sometimes you also know what they are going to do where they are going. Most of these Facebookers share photos of the places they visit. They also post pictures of their mode of transport, particularly if they travel by air. On top of that, they don't hesitate to post pictures of their hosts, at times without their hosts' permission. Sojourners are wonderful people because they trust their friends, and don't suspect them of witchcraft.

The joke-tellers make issues lighter. Some of them retell the jokes that they have heard somewhere, and others compose their own jokes. They are good because they make you laugh and relax. Their primary problem is that they sometimes concentrate on telling jokes at the expense of serious business. They don't draw a line between joke telling and serious life business. When you go to them looking for advice, they tell you a joke that might not help solve your problem.

Silent killers don't say a thing about what they read on Facebook. They don't comment on anything. They don't wish anyone, "Happy birthday." You even don't know if they are active Facebookers or not. Like, the invisible spirits, you just sense that they are there in the background. They watch you from a distance. They are lukewarm because they neither affirm your posts nor criticize them. They make no enemies on Facebook. Their main weakness is that they don't share their knowledge, assuming that they have it. They contribute nothing because they either think that they are superior to others or they consider themselves too dull to contribute anything. They deprive others of their wisdom, yet they benefit from other people's wisdom. My sons, a good facebooker writes relevant comments on his friends' posts, and wishes them well on their birthdays.

The philosophers are also known as the "one-minute wisdom people" who bombard their friends with wisdom sayings that they compose themselves or borrow from others. Although some of those quotable quotes are philosophical and helpful, they are sometimes too abstract. They lack the applicability and simplicity that are needed in real life experiences. Of course, their wise sayings do inspire, but they are far divorced from the usual human life.

Human life is built on the daily experiences of both success and failure, not on utopian morality. People appreciate wise sayings that one has composed rather than wisdom sayings that have been copied from someone else. This "copy and paste" wisdom prevents many from being original thinkers. Remember, philosophers aren't created from borrowing other people's wisdom, but from learning others' wisdom for the purpose of manufacturing one's own. Wise quotes may be tempting, but they might be bereft of any significance to your readers unless they are yours.

The birthday people appear on Facebook once in a year, particularly on the day that follows their birthdays. Their primary purpose on Facebook is to read the birthdays wishes that their friends would have written on their walls. Most of these people are grateful for the birthday wishes posted by their friends. They usually thank the friends either individually or generally. Some have the tendency to thank their close friends individually, and other friends as a group. Once they show their appreciation, they disappear for another twelve months. They only reappear on the day after their next birthday. They are very nice people, but they miss the fact that birthday messages should be reciprocated.

The "golden mean" people are balanced people. They are involved in Facebook friendship in a balanced manner. They publish their feelings without trying to make the whole world sympathize with them. They post their wisdom, but they also appreciate other people's wisdom. They post opinions, but they also comment on other people's postings. They discuss soccer, politics, relationships, current affairs, and so on, without being fanatics of only one field. They don't pretend to know everything, yet they don't hide their knowledge. They talk about God without trying to convert anybody on Facebook. They give testimonies about the doings of God in their lives without exaggerating. They share their sorrows and happiness, but in a manner that allows others to empathize with them.

They share their pictures, not as a way of proving themselves to be more beautiful than all their friends, but to immortalize certain moments in their lives. They tell jokes, but their postings don't revolve around joke-telling only. They write about politics, but they know that politics isn't a preserve of a few people. They write about love, but they don't pretend to be the only people who know what love is. They celebrate the successes of their children without trying to prove that theirs are better than their friends' children. They wish all their friends well on their birthdays. These people have stricken a balance in their Facebook interactions. My sons, aspire to be the "golden mean" facebookers.

My sons, make friends. Take care of your friends, and allow them to take care of you. But don't influence your friends to do what's evil. Respect your friends. Reciprocate their love. Never turn your back to a friend in need. A person can lose his brothers, sisters, and parents, but will always have friends. The best thing about friends is that you choose them, please, do so wisely.

Generosity and Gratitude

Kusatenda uroyi (Lack of gratitude is evil).
Kandiro kanopfumba kunobva kamwe (Generosity should be reciprocated).

My sons, in our society, people have different gifts, talents, power, influence, and resources. The capitalist ideology that most countries have embraced as the hallmark of good economic governance ensures that there is competition for the scarce resources that human beings need for survival. This competition for scarce resources brings about stiff competition for political, economic, and military dominance of other nations by the super powers. Those individuals and countries that are more competitive than others are better placed to acquire more of the world's scarce resources than the less competitive.

However, despite the economic disparities between individuals or nations, human beings depend on each other. There are very few people or countries, if any at all, that are economically and financially self-sufficient. People and countries depend on each other, and consequently need each other. That interdependence shows the extent to which people and countries need to assist each other in times of need. This natural interdependence compels people and countries to learn the art of empathy, generosity, and gratitude.

Even within one country, people have different stations and professions in this life because all of us can't be the same. If all people were cooks, there would be no farmers, and, therefore, no food to cook. If all persons were professors, there would be no students to teach. Although all professions are important, and do complement each other in one way or another, the human society has placed more importance and value on some professions at the expense of others. Hence, employers are willing to pay more for the services offered by some professionals than by others. That leads to remuneration discrepancies. The wage that one receives depends on the value the society places on the job one does, and on the principle of supply and demand. If there are too many people looking for the same kind of job, the demand and wages for such workers drop. If we have very few people qualified to perform a particular job, the demand for such professionals rises, and so does the remuneration.

Naturally, each country's economy should enable its citizens to lead a decent life. But it doesn't always happen that way. There is an unequal distribution of almost every nation's wealth. There is unemployment too, which impoverishes many people despite their eagerness to find a job and earn a living. Sometimes, there is also exploitation by employers that prevents those who are lucky to get employment from acquiring a fair share of their country's wealth. The result of that unemployment and exploitation is poverty. Poverty is a reality, my sons, and most of it isn't caused by laziness.

There will always be some people who struggle to make ends meet notwithstanding the economic boom in their country of citizenship. Some people will never have enough to eat in spite of their relentless toils. I know of people who have two or more jobs, yet they struggle to make ends meet. It should never cross your mind that poverty is always a consequence of laziness, or that richness is a result of hard work. Some people have everything that they need in life, not because they worked hard for it, but because they are better positioned in society. The world is full of people who inherited their wealth from their ancestors, yet they brag about having worked so hard to acquire their wealth. Yes, their ancestors might have worked hard, but that's their ancestors' sweat not theirs. Those who inherit their ancestors' wealth aren't hard workers at all, but are mere privileged beneficiaries.

My sons, poverty is sometimes an inescapable reality. Never scold or belittle anybody for being impecunious. Yes, Mother Earth has enough wealth for everyone, but sometimes human greed, selfishness, and exploitation prevent everyone to get a fair share from their country's resources.

My sons, most of the poverty in this world is undeserved. Consequently, most poor people should never be blamed for their poverty. More often than not, the poor are victims of human avarice, individualism, indifference, and selfishness. The plight of the poor calls for all human beings to think of the attitudes and behaviors that unfairly enrich the minority while impoverishing the majority. The poor need redemption.

My sons, play your part in alleviating the plight of the poor. Learn the art of generosity. Generosity is the ability to think and take care of other people's needs even if one doesn't have enough for himself and his immediate family. It's the willingness to acknowledge that the world's wealth was created for all of us, and no one should be deprived of his share. My sons, you should learn to share the little that you have with those who are less privileged.

However, I want you to know that giving away anything to anyone isn't easy. Human beings are naturally selfish and greedy. Giving is an art that must be learnt. If you wish to learn the art of generosity, start with small things, such as used shirts, trousers, books, plates, blankets, and so on. The art of giving can be acquired by progressing from humble beginnings. Learn to eradicate poverty and misery in your own little ways. Much of the poverty-induced suffering in this world is unjustified, because it can be prevented if privileged people were willing to share what they have.

My sons, learn to share what you have with those who are in need because that's what human beings should do. Of course, it's painful to give away anything initially, but once you get into the habit of giving, you will realize the pleasure that you derive from it, and you will never stop giving. There is greater pleasure in sharing your blessings with the less privileged than in hoarding them. Our people have a proverb that says, "*Kupa huvigisa*," which can be translated literarily as "giving is banking." If you learn to give, you will never be in want. The more you give away, the more blessings you receive.

My sons, I want you to know that I am a beneficiary of the generosity of many people who I have encountered throughout my life. Every time that I think of where I started in life, the journey that I have traveled, and where I am now, I don't doubt the efficacy and miraculous touch of generosity. No single day passes by, without me thinking of those heroes and heroines of my life. There are many times that I pray for more wealth and a better paying job, not for my own benefit, but so that I can help those many people who assisted me in making my dream come true. I would like you to know that sharing your wealth with the needy can break the cycle of poverty, because had it not been for the sacrifices of other people, I wouldn't have managed to give you the type of life that you have. I want you to know that you owe the opportunities that you have, not only to me or your mother, but also to the many people who assisted us in one way or another throughout our life journeys. Whenever I think of those generous people, I am motivated to share what I have with those who are less fortunate even though it hurts.

My greatest setback is that I don't have enough resources to be able to fulfill all my dreams, but I am convinced that one day, a miracle will happen, and some of my dreams will be fulfilled. My sons, my advice and encouragement to you is that; learn to give until it hurts. When you get promoted at your work, don't only think of purchasing expensive cars, or building mansions, but also think of the difference that you would make to other people's lives by giving away some of that wealth.

You don't need to possess a mountain of gold to be able to share with the less privileged, but a human heart. You need empathy. When I came to Texas in 2012, and got a part-time job as a teaching instructor, the man who volunteered to give me a ride to where I lived, at 10:00 pm, after class, twice per week, had a very old pick-up that had seen better days, and most probably, better owners. I could tell that he was a poor man, but he had a big heart. Most of the time, the good man had to persuade the tired truck to start up. Whenever he dropped me off at the house where we lived, I prayed that the truck would be able to take him back to his home, safely. I was touched by the sacrifice that he was making for me—for us. Every time he gave me a ride, he would tell me how happy he was to be able to do something for me.

Beneficiaries of generosity come in different shapes and shades. If you decide to learn the art of generosity, you would meet three basic kinds of recipients: the ungrateful, the corrupt, and the thankful. I have experienced all the three kinds of recipients.

Starting with the ungrateful, I want you to know that some people will never say, "thank you," for whatever good you do for them. I know how discouraging it is to make sacrifices for people, or giving away things to people who will never show their gratitude. Lack of appreciation is painful to the giver because human beings, by their very nature, desire to be thanked. Thankfulness raises their spirits and makes them want to do more for others. Thankfulness is like what fuel is to a vehicle; it gives it the power to move on despite the rough terrain of the road ahead. Gratitude does to the heart what rain does to the dry soil—it makes it softer, more pliable, more fertile, and more fruitful.

The ability to show or express gratitude isn't a virtue that every beneficiary of other people's generosity possesses. Why? There is no definite answer to that. First, it could be that some people were never taught how to say, "thank you," in the families in which they were born and raised. It could be that nobody appreciated anybody in their families. So, the children never had the opportunity to learn the art of thankfulness since most children learn through observation.

Second, I also think that some people don't show gratitude because of selfishness. In their selfish minds, they begrudge the giver for not giving them more than was offered. In fact, they resent the giver and intend to teach him a lesson in giving more, by withholding the expected "thank you." Their ingratitude is intended to show their dissatisfaction.

Third, some people forget to say thank you because they think that it doesn't matter. They have never given anything to anybody, and consequently, haven't tested the sweetness of being thanked. They don't know how much their ingratitude affects the giver.

Fourth, some people don't think that it's necessary to verbalize their thankfulness. These people are grateful deep inside themselves, and they believe that unverbalized gratitude is good enough. They don't realize that their gratitude is intended for the giver, not for themselves, so it has to be verbalized. The Shona people have a proverb that says, "*kutenda kwekiti kuri mumoyo,*" which means that the cat's gratitude is in its heart. This proverb is unhelpful to those who want to learn to verbally thank their benefactors.

Your gratitude might be as deep as the ocean, but unless it's verbally expressed, it's usually interpreted as ingratitude. Such people take it for granted that the provider should know that they are grateful, but since they don't say it, the giver may never know of their thankfulness. If you want to thank somebody, do it now and do it openly.

Finally, for anyone to be able to thank any giver, he or she should be humble enough to do that. Without humility, one can never be able to say, "thank you." Gratitude is a virtue of the humble. The proud will never be able to thank anybody because to thank somebody is to acknowledge the importance of the gift and the dependence the receiver has upon the giver. It's also to recognize that without the gift, things wouldn't be the same for the receiver. The proud recipient may not want to accept the fact that he can't make it alone in life; he needs others.

But, should you stop giving because of such recipients? My response is, "no." For the sake of those few that show their gratitude, continue to provide for the less privileged. Don't allow the ungrateful receivers to dampen your spirits. Yes, in cases where you can educate them about showing gratitude, please, don't hesitate. Remind them, if they forget. Encourage them, if they hesitate. And thank them for thanking you.

My sons, you will meet corrupt beneficiaries, who upon receiving your gift, would in turn, misappropriate it. I don't intend to teach you to dictate how the recipients should use the gifts that you offer them, but this group is worth mentioning. These recipients would thank you for your generosity, but would misappropriate the donation. If you give them clothes, sometimes they sell them for very little money. If you give them money, they squander it loosely and irresponsibly. Sometimes, you give these people money, and they use it to buy something that's destructive to their health, such as drugs or alcohol. That's why some people offer food to beggars rather than money, which I don't agree with, as I shall explain later.

One such receiver disappointed me. What happened is that there was a time when we assisted orphans in the rural village where I was born, with school uniforms, writing books, pens, and tuition fees. One of the boys, who gratefully received those gifts, instead of using them appropriately, he sold everything and went down to South Africa in search for a job. Although searching for a job was a good thing, the money that I had given him was for school fees, not for bus fare. If he had told me in the first place that he needed bus fare to South Africa, I would have given him the bus fare, and then offered the uniform and books to someone else, who wanted to use them.

Some people misrepresent their status in the community so that they can receive gifts that are intended for the poor, and would then sell them to the poor. That was the case with some of the food handouts that were given out in the rural villages in Zimbabwe by some non-governmental organizations. Some wealthy and influential members of the community deprived the deserving poor beneficiaries of the food that could have alleviated their poverty. So, my sons, when you give to the poor, make sure that your gifts get to the intended beneficiaries.

Despite the rotten eggs that you will encounter in the generosity basket, there are many good eggs that you will find in the same basket too. My sons, some people, are thankful. Their gratitude can humble you, and may make you cry. There are many people out there who do acknowledge and appreciate the generosity that they have experienced throughout their lives. Some of them go a step further by learning to share their gifts with the less fortunate whenever they can. They also work so hard so that they can reciprocate the generosity that they received. Such recipients make the giver want to give away more.

My sons, there are many times when the business of giving seems unrewarding, but that shouldn't prevent you from giving. The many people who appreciate the gifts that they receive should encourage you to continue providing for others as much as your means permit. You should avoid certain things and attitudes when you give away anything. First, neither expect to be thanked, nor demand gratitude from the receiver. Let thankfulness come to you as a surprise and a gift. A gift that comes as a surprise really humbles the receiver. In addition to that, if you don't expect to be thanked, and then you aren't acknowledged, the lack of gratitude won't upset you. Yes, you may gently remind a person to be grateful, once or twice, but if ingratitude is his or her habit, don't waste your time.

Second, when you give away anything, don't expect any reciprocity. There are many people you are going to help who have nothing with which they can reciprocate your generosity. Yes, they have a "thank you," but don't expect it either, because they may choose to withhold it due to selfishness or other reasons. A giver should never solicit for reciprocity, for it should come out of the receiver's free will. Generosity isn't barter trade.

Third, it's very important to remember that when you give out money to anybody who is asking for it, don't dictate how the receiver is going to use that money, unless the purpose was included in the request. For instance, if you give someone some money for school fees, then you must demand that the money is used for school fees, and not for something else. But if someone asks for money without telling you how he wants to use it, and you decide to give him the money, don't dictate how the receiver is going to use that cash. You don't have the right to take away someone's right to decide what to do with the money that he receives, just because you are the donor. Yes, give, but don't dehumanize the receiver. A person might be a beggar, but she still has the right to make her own personal decisions. What if they buy drugs using your money? That's none of the donor's business, as long as that wasn't communicated to him when the request was made.

Finally, if you give someone something, don't try to subjugate that person. The fact that you have given someone something doesn't warrant you to abuse him. Never use your generosity to buy loyalty or favors. I have met people who would give you something with the intention of oppressing you afterwards. Such donors make you pay back in one way or the other. When I was in seminary, a colleague gave me a pair of sandals and a T-shirt. After a few weeks, I had to give them back because I felt that he was using his generosity to take away my freedom. My sons, I have learned that at times, it's better to wallow in poverty than to accept a gift that takes away your freedom. It's better to die a destitute but with your freedom, than to enjoy a life of abundance as a bonded slave.

After all is said, I remain a believer in generosity, and I know that this world would never be the same if more and more people were generous. I am aware that there are many miracles that people who give to charity perform every day. These miracles do change lives for the better. I also know that there are many people who hold on to their wealth while other people starve. If people wanted, they could turn this world into a paradise.

My sons, our people have a proverb that says, "*Kusatenda uroyi,*" which literally means that an ungrateful person is a witch. A witch is a person who uses secret, evil, and mysterious powers to harm others. Ingratitude is equivalent to witchcraft because it kills the flame of generosity in the giver. Witchcraft kills the body, but ingratitude kills the spirit.

Wherever you go, don't forget to thank people for the good that they do or have done for you. All people want to be thanked, and never be found wanting in that respect. The golden phrase, "Thank you," must ever be on your lips. In this world, you will never run short of people to appreciate because we depend on each other. If you don't value the gift, then thank the giver for the love with which he would have offered you the gift. Don't go to bed before you thank the person who deserves to be thanked.

Charity begins at home. Start with us your parents. There are many sacrifices that we have made, and continue to make for you, for which we deserve a "thank you." They say, "Familiarity breeds contempt," but this should never be allowed to happen in any family. We should be thanked for bringing you into this world without being obliged to. Your mother spent nine, dangerous months nurturing you in her womb. My sons, the experience of giving birth isn't only excruciating, but also life-threatening. Your mother endured both, so that you could safely come into this world. She suckled you from her breasts and dandled you on her hips, for many months. She is special. Every mother is remarkable and sacred. Every mother deserves to be respected and appreciated.

My sons, don't forget your mother either in your times of plenty, or of need. Your mom, just like other human beings, has her misgivings, some of which you know and others you don't, but she remains your mother. Don't hold that against her. Don't publish your mother's mistakes to the world, because the world has no sympathy for someone who demonizes his or her own mother. My sons, stand by your mother's side whenever she needs your support. When you have to correct her, do it with the respect and love that she deserves. Thank your mother, not only in words, but also in deeds. There is nothing as vivid and convincing as a "thank you" that has been dramatized in deeds.

Your mother needs your gratitude for raising you up. She spent countless sleepless nights trying to comfort you. Some of those sleepless nights were spent in hospitals when you were sick. She toils in the fields and industries in order to bring food to the table.

My sons, don't forget the many, and long prayers she unceasingly offers for you. The way you treat her should always reflect your gratitude for all she has done for you. Let your mother find a protector and benefactor in you. In our culture, neglecting one's mother isn't only an insult to the community, but also to the ancestors. And please, don't insult the ancestors, for they retaliate.

Thank me, your father, just like you thank your mother. Refuse to be turned against me because of domestic politics. Some mothers have a way of turning their children against their father. I am glad that your mom doesn't subscribe to such divisive politics. My sons, fathers too need to be loved. Remember the sleepless nights I spent in order to make you happy. Remember the lonely weekends I spent in trying to save enough money for your education. I might have been stricter with you, but I had to be, so that you would be the fine young men that you have become. Every father has the responsibility of molding his sons into fine citizens of the world. Never resent those times when I suppressed signs of rebellion and mischief in you. I had to do it because that's the responsibility of every father.

Thank me, for taming you into fine gentlemen. People are born brutes just like other animals, but their significant others, and society have an obligation to transform them into human beings. It's easier for some people to remain savages because that's the way all people are born. It's the duty of every father to assist his children to become law-abiding citizens.

My sons, you must know that the noble responsibility of raising children sometimes demands that I conceal my love from you. Never mistake that concealment of my love, for the lack of it because I can only love as a father should. The divinely instituted duties of every father demand that he does what a father has to do. If you carefully look beyond my words and actions, you would see the mountains of love that I have for you. Every father has to choose between being his sons' best friend, or being his sons' best father. I chose the latter. So, my boys, don't mistake me for your friend because I am not. I am your father, and I can only love like a father can.

Every man grows older and becomes weaker. Presently, I might appear to be invincible, at least to you, but you should know that no man remains indomitable. A time shall come, and indeed it's almost upon me, when I shall be frail and in need of your care and love. When that time comes, please, don't desert me. There are many misdemeanors that can be committed against one's father and can be forgiven, but neglecting or beating up your dad is unforgivable. It upsets not only the community, but also the ancestors of the land. I need to be thanked for all the sacrifices that I have made for you. I also thank you for being pliable members of this family.

My sons, learn to say "Thank you," to your teachers. Teachers are the people with whom you spent most of your time when you were young. Although I played a significant role in molding you into the persons you are now; teachers also played a significant role that I couldn't have performed with equal grace. In most countries, teachers work under poor working conditions, yet they never lose heart and hope in assisting their students to achieve the best results, both in academics and life. Many teachers work under extremely dehumanizing conditions such as low salary and poor housing, yet they continue to sacrifice their time to give you the extra push that you need to be the professional that you ought to be. Sometimes, they were stricter with you because they wanted you to be the best you could become; never count that against them. Remember, they too are human beings, and they sometimes make mistakes in the way they instruct you, but never count that against them later in life.

My sons, here, I am not talking about teachers who turn into criminals, and abuse the children placed under their care. Criminals should be treated like criminals. I am talking of the well-intentioned, but overzealous teachers, who because of their passion for their duties, sometimes overdo things. Never begrudge a teacher unless she or she is a criminal.

Gratitude that's shown to a teacher will encourage all of them to work harder, more diligently, and more efficiently. I spent most of my professional life as a teacher, and I encountered students who said, "thank you," and students who had no "thank you," in their vocabulary. Gratitude that comes from a student changes the mood of the teacher. It complements the meager salaries that teachers earn. It brings a smile to the teacher's face, and purpose to the teacher's sacrifices. Just send them a message saying, "thank you." Most of your teachers can be found on Facebook and other social media. Just say, "thank you."

You must always remember to thank your friends for all the good things they have done and continue to do for you. Sometimes we take for granted what our friends do for us. Our friends make sacrifices for us. Respect them. Love them, and let them know that you will sacrifice your time for their wellbeing. Show your gratitude to them in words and deeds.

My sons, if you become employers, you must thank all your workers for the work they do. You can do that by providing them with safe working conditions. Yes, they may be poor and desperate for a job, but you must always remember that they are human beings. Treat them with dignity. Let them know that you value what they do. Don't be afraid to praise them openly, beginning with those who do the least valued jobs. You should always remember that a human being shouldn't be valued according to the job that he or she does. She might be a toilet cleaner, but she isn't the toilet that she cleans. He might be your cook, but he isn't the pot in which he cooks. Show your appreciation for what every one of your employees does. If the need to reprimand one of them arises, do it with compassion and respect. Praise them for their good works and sacrifices. There is nothing as pleasing to the soul as a good word about one's good work coming from the employer. A "thank you," coming from the employer invokes the kind of motivation that money might not be able to ignite in the employee.

If you happen to be someone's employee, you must also show your gratitude to your employer. This can be done by doing your work honestly and professionally. Try to do better all the time you perform your task. You must deserve the salary that you get from your employer. You also ought to thank him or her openly for allowing you to work for his or her company. Once in a while, write a letter to your employer chronicling all your gratitude.

When corrected, don't take it personal because correction will make you a better worker. Employers may rather put up with a less productive worker who shows gratitude and the eagerness to learn than an exceptionally skilled worker who is pompous and ungrateful. A thankful person can be molded into a highly skillful worker, but there is no improvement you can do to a thankless and I-know-it-all worker.

If you will have children, teach them to say, "thank you." Never allow your children to be found wanting in that respect. A sincere thank you makes even selfish people generous. There are many gifts that we receive and for which we can't reciprocate, but the only thing that we can do is to thank the giver. If you get a gift that you don't like, at least, you should thank the giver for the love with which she would have given you the gift. My sons, teach your children to thank people because they will never be in want. Nothing is as disgraceful and annoying as a thankless person.

Thank your neighbors for all the little things they do for you. They watch your home when you are at work. They wish you well even without you knowing it. If you wrong any of your neighbors, ask for forgiveness. Thank strangers for being kind to you. Thank everyone who deserves it. Don't lose the opportunity to show your gratitude whenever the opportunity presents itself.

My sons, learn to thank people. Many times, the only way you can reciprocate people's goodness to you is by thanking them. Don't hesitate to thank people because you lose nothing in doing so. He who hesitates to thank others is a fool. Let appreciation flow like a stream from your heart. Be generous. Give out to the less privileged as much as you can. Plough back into the community. No one has ever gained wealth without the use and help of other people; remember those people. Stay away from individualism, selfishness, and greed. A man's wealth isn't measured by the delicious food that he eats, the expensive clothes that he wears, the luxury cars he drives, or the mansion in which he lives, but by the amount of wealth that he shares with those who struggle to make ends meet. A better man knows that this world would be inhabitable if he had no neighbors.

Decision-Making

Mazvokuda mavanga enyora (If you make bad decisions, you would suffer the consequences).
Chidamoyo, zamo kumera pambabvu (People's choices should be respected even if the choices seem poor).

My sons, times will come that will demand that you make your own decisions. That's one of our callings as adults. When you were young, we made most choices for you, using our own experiences as guidelines, but as you mature, you will need to make your own decisions. The willingness to make decisions is the evidence that one accepts to take the responsibility for his life. The older you become, the more serious decisions you are expected to make. That's the nature of life, and no adult can escape that.

When you were young, we chose clothes for you. But now that you have become adults, you will be expected to choose your own fashion and clothes to wear. Whatever clothes you choose, make sure that it's decent and acceptable in the society in which you are a member. Some styles that are acceptable in one society might not be acceptable in other places, and you should respect that. Whatever types of trousers you go for, never wear them below your waist or bottom like what we sometimes see some young men doing, because it isn't only nauseating and repulsive, but also abominable, to say the least. According to our culture, there is nothing on your butts that's worth showing to the people. A man has two options: to wear his trousers the normal way or to take it off and then walk around naked. That behavior takes away from you more than it gives you. Shouldn't one wear clothes the way he wants? Can anyone prescribe the kind of clothes one should wear without violating that person's right to freedom of choice? My sons, you should also be aware that the pursuit of your rights mustn't violate other people's rights. Dress appropriately, and as dictated by the occasion in which you find yourself.

You will also choose a profession, and that isn't an easy decision for most young men. Choosing the right profession is vital because, in most cases, you will stay in your job for an extended time. Although it's possible to change your job, it takes some doing to do that. Therefore, you have to choose the right profession; otherwise, your working life will be miserable. Getting a good job is a result of a deliberate pursuit of a good academic or training program. A good educational program is the one that will enable you to bring food to the table after graduation.

Yes, you might have a degree program that attracts your heart, but I say to you, go for the one that will enable you to feed your family. You may still pursue your hobbies, on the sidelines of your chosen degree program, but unless that hobby will bring food to your table, please, let it complement your primary profession. You don't want to spend many years studying for a degree, and then fail to get a job after graduation. Before you opt for a degree program, do your research. You will find a lot of information concerning employable degree programs on the internet. There are also many people who are willing to give you valuable career guidance about that. So, please take advantage of that.

The other issue concerning the choice of your degree program and profession is that, you are strangers in an alien land, and some employers have challenges in employing aliens. Never be fooled to believe that racism is an issue of the past because it doesn't die easily. If you want to be on the safe side, pursue a profession that will compel employers to find it difficult to segregate against you. Go for a profession that will bear witness to your capabilities as an employee, without you begging to get employment. You might ask me why I chose to become a teacher and theologian. My sons, where I was born and bred, the only profession we knew about was that of teaching, nursing, and policing. In order to get into a nursing school, you needed to know someone who knew someone, who knew some influential people. I wasn't that lucky. At the high school where I was schooled, there were only two qualified teachers—the headmaster and the Math teacher. I never had the opportunities and options that you have. Life was a struggle to make ends meet.

In the four years I spent at that high school, I only got a pair of shoes at the end of my third year. Those who know the point at which I started the marathon of life will bear witness to that. I have achieved more than I ever dreamt I would achieve in a lifetime. My sons, don't mistake a hobby for a profession because a hobby doesn't need to bring food to your table, but a profession should. Before you think of pursuing a hobby for a profession, make sure that you have food on your table.

You will also decide on who shall be your friends. Friends are imperative in this world, and you will make many. Unfortunately, many times, we don't choose our friends, but we just become friends. Although you may not have much awareness as to how you find friends, you have much control concerning who become your friends. Friends are important because they are outsiders and as such, they widen your worldview. They have different stories and ways of telling them. Good friends can be an excellent source of knowledge. You can depend on them, and them on you. But never allow friends to change the person you are unless it will benefit you, or make you a better person.

Bad friends can influence you negatively and therefore, turning you into an evil person. Make your friends proud of you by contributing positively to the friendship. Don't befriend a person who does drugs. You shouldn't be found in the company of criminals. Don't stay in the company of people who encourage you to abscond from classes, or not doing your homework. Don't allow your friends to do the thinking for you. Take every piece of advice they offer you with a pinch of salt. Don't blame your failures on them. Take responsibility over your actions.

Your decision making will also be demanded in the area of food. Sooner or later, you will cook for yourself, which I think is the easiest thing to do, and the hardest being choosing what to cook. Not everything that is edible is worth eating. Get the knowledge about the kind of food that isn't harmful to the body. Some foods are harmful to your health and also addictive. Avoid them.

This advice also applies to drinking. Drink what you wish to drink, but don't overdo it. If you choose to drink alcohol, you should do it responsibly. Some alcoholic beverages are hazardous to health, and their producers don't hide that fact. Don't drink alcohol and drive. The temptation to drink and drive is compulsive, but the consequences are devastating. If you do, you will end up either in jail, or in the grave. You don't win either way. If you cause someone's injury or death because of your reckless driving, there are two prisons involved—society's prison and your conscience. There are many things that can send one to jail, but driving under the influence of alcohol shouldn't be one of them. Never allow any alcoholic drink to become your master. Be in charge. You should know when to say, "no" to an offer of a drink.

My sons don't smoke tobacco. I have said this before, but it's worth repeating. Don't even decide to try it. Smoking isn't only dangerous to your own health, but also to other people's. Most individuals who smoke are continuing to find themselves being ostracized by the society each day. More stringent and unfriendly laws are passed and implemented, and the person who smokes finds that upsetting. In addition to that smoking is addictive. It's better and easier to fight the habit before it enslaves you. I foresee a situation where some people who smoke would be discriminated against in jobs, housing, sports, and other places in the human society. It has already started.

One good thing about smoking is that, you don't know how it feels unless you start smoking. You will never feel the need to smoke until you start smoking and get hooked to the habit. Smoking is one of the human habits that don't come to your house, and beg you to embrace them. It doesn't grab you by the arm and twist it to force you to be a disciple. You invite it upon yourself. It's like inviting an elephant into your one-roomed house only to find yourself being pushed outside. There are many smokers who regret having decided to do it in the first place. Don't become one of them. A life full of regrets isn't pleasant. Don't try it, lest you get hooked.

Yes, you will have to marry one day because that's expected of every man in our culture. When the time comes, please, choose a woman you love, and with whom you are ready to explore the vicissitudes of life for a lifetime. Marriage is supposed to be permanent. It's also a mystery of forgiveness, and unless you are prepared to forgive and be forgiven, you won't stay in it longer. The first is the dating, then the romance, then the wedding, and the rest are lots of compromises and forgiveness. Finding a compatible partner isn't a simple task, but you can always find someone who is willing to explore the secrets of life with you.

Please, don't choose to impregnate a woman unless you are willing to take the responsibility for the consequences. If a woman rejects your proposal, don't lose sleep over it. Don't die for it. There is always someone who is losing sleep over you. Hunt for her. Don't begrudge a woman for breaking up with you, for it's sometimes a blessing in disguise. Those who are destined for each other can never escape each other's reach. Sometimes, a marriage doesn't work out for you; please, try harder. If the relationship doesn't improve, please, let go. Some challenges are resolved by letting go than holding on. Some problems are solved by parting ways than sticking together. Better part ways than live in a hell of an abusive or loveless union. But before that last goodbye, try your best to reconcile.

In making your decisions, there are many people who are ready to advise you on how to make them. There is nothing wrong in seeking other people's advice. What's wrong is to allow other people to make life-changing decisions for you. Every decision comes with consequences, and these are better faced by the one who takes a measure of responsibility for his decisions. Decision making isn't easy because it involves taking risks. Don't force some people to make decisions for you so that when things go wrong, you have someone to blame. Please, own your decisions and accept full responsibility for them. That's what adults do. You may ask for advice from experts, but at the end of the day, make your own decisions. Own them. People who over-depend on professional or other people's advice never learn to take full responsibility for the consequences of their decisions. There is greater joy in celebrating the fruits of one's decisions, and greater lessons to be learnt from one's mistakes.

When making decisions, always think of both advantages and disadvantages of choosing to walk that path. Don't allow excitement to prevent you from seeing the joys and sorrows of choosing one path and not the other. Be prepared for what might go wrong because sometimes things do go wrong. This preparedness will protect you from shock if your decision bears bitter fruits. But don't be afraid to take risks. Risk-taking is a part of life that shouldn't be avoided. However, that doesn't mean that you don't have to prepare for adverse consequences most of the time.

My sons, when you were young, we compelled you to attend our church because you couldn't choose a church for yourselves. Now that you are becoming men, it's your responsibility to choose your own church or parish. You might choose not to remain Christians and Catholics; it's up to you. Be that as it may, I wish you would remain Catholics. As a Catholic myself, I believe that it's one of the best churches in the world, but the decision is yours to make. I discovered that myself, and I encourage you to learn about Catholicism and discover it's richness by yourselves.

Respect all churches, for there is no denomination that's holier than the other. All churches have both saints and sinners. All churches are the same, for they seek to do what's good. They aim to be channels of God's blessings to humankind. They all try to transform this world by teaching their members to observe the principles of the Gospel of Jesus Christ, of love, peace, tolerance, respect, liberation, equality, and joy. Their teachings help mold people into good citizens of both this world and the world to come.

My sons, it isn't easy to choose a church because there are so many churches around, and each one of them claims to be better than the other. Of course, I have my bias towards Catholicism. Churches do have different doctrines and beliefs, but their mission is the same. Once you choose your church, you should learn its history, traditions, and rituals. You should actively participate in your church's activities. Learn to pray in the manner your church teaches you to pray. Sing with other church members. Read the bible, for most of them do.

Please, attend church services, but never allow your church to enslave you. Going to church isn't the only obligation a good Christian has, for there are many others. In addition to attending church services, God needs you to do what's right, by unwaveringly observing his commandments, helping the poor and less privileged, loving and respecting your neighbor, and taking care of your family. You should create time to attend church services, although nobody should force you to do it. Sometimes, you will miss church services, and that's part of life. If you miss a church service, don't despair because God knows where you live and all your challenges. He will come home looking for you.

My sons, never be hypocrites. A hypocrite is a person who claims to be who he isn't. A hypocrite condemns others for the things that he wouldn't condemn himself for doing. He is a person who sees a stick that's in his neighbor's eye, without being concerned about a log that's in his own eye. Try your best to be a good person, and to keep the rules of your church. Don't judge those who try and fail, but assist them if you can. Never consider yourselves better than other people just because you are a Christian. You should know that there are many good people who don't go to church. Respect all people.

My sons, don't overdo church things. Pray, but don't exaggerate because God already knows your challenges and wishes, even before you pray. Pay your tithes, but never overdo it because your financial obligation is first and foremost to your family. Sing, but never do it to excess because heaven is full of angelic musicians that can sing better than you. Dance, but not to the extent King David is said to have reached because he was a king, and you aren't. Don't monopolize church ministries because God gave you brothers and sisters. Allow other Christians to participate in church activities because that's what God wants.

You are free to choose your own religion. However, if given a choice between being a believer and not, please choose believing. If given a choice between God and nothing, please, opt for God. There are many challenges that human beings face, which can only be understood and resolved through faith in God.

My sons, some decisions, are difficult to make, and once they are made, there is no going back. Some decisions become easier to make through experience, but you should always remember that experience isn't a magnificent teacher. It teaches you a lesson after you will have made a mistake, and some errors have fatal consequences. Don't be indecisive because that, in itself, is deciding not to do anything. Make decisions, but please, let them be informed by reason. Don't just anticipate positive results from your decisions because almost every decision has a consequence that has two sides, and you should expect either side. So, make your own decisions. Own them. And be ready to take responsibility for their consequences. Never allow the wrong decisions that you made in the past to hold you back and prevent you from moving forward in life. Learn from your mistakes.

The Importance of Education

Kusaziva hufa (Lack of knowledge is as bad as death).
Kure kwegava ndokusina mutsubvu (If you want to achieve something, you have to persevere).

My sons, there is no substitute for education. Grab every opportunity that comes your way to educate yourselves. There are many ways in which you can pursue this noble endeavor, one of which is to go to school, college, or university. In these institutions, there are experts who know how to give you the right doses of knowledge. You will meet professionals, some of whom have dedicated their entire lives to sharing their knowledge with people who seek to learn.

If you go to a college, do respect your professors. In college, you will have an obligation to write assignments and participate in class discussions. Play your part. Where you don't understand, never hesitate to ask the professor for clarification. Meet all assignment deadlines, and where you can't meet them, request for some grace period from the professor. Make the request in advance. Never miss classes unless circumstances beyond your control force you to. Many professors don't think highly of students who miss classes. Never cheat on a test because that will count heavily on you when you get caught. Of course, you may be successful in cheating in a test, but you will face the consequences when you get a job where you are required to use the skills that you wouldn't have mastered in college.

Observe classroom etiquette. Don't listen to music or browse your cell phone while the class is in progress because that's disrespectful to the professor and other students. Most professors may quickly forgive you for failing to understand some of the concepts and skills that they teach you, but might find it hard to forgive your disrespect to them or other students. Remember to turn off your phone, and keep it away from your sight. Resist the temptation to turn it on.

In a college or university, you will study with other students. It's good that God gave you colleagues. They too should be respected. Never engage in any classroom behavior that will distract your classmates from pursuing their academic goals. No to bullying. Respect your classmates' views even if they differ from yours. If you are required to critique them, do it with grace and respect. You should learn to separate ideas from persons. A person might nurse some bad academic opinion, but it doesn't make him a bad person. Learn to criticize the idea, but not the person. Never take your opinion as the final word because it isn't. There are many other ways of looking at issues, and you should remember that yours is only one of them.

If you actively participate in class discussions, expect both affirmation and criticism from your classmates. Never take their constructive criticism personally, but you should use it to perfect your opinions. If your classmate offers a more intelligible and logical view, please, don't hesitate to give her or him the credit. It's noble to give credit where it's due.

Don't be afraid to change your views if need be, for human beings should grow in their wisdom. Although convictions should be firm, they shouldn't be cast in iron. Learn to take a firm stance and defend what you believe in, until you are convinced that there is another better way of looking at the same issue. Sometimes, better opinions come from the least expected people—give everyone a chance. The greatest asset in all this, is learning how to listen without being judgmental. Those who have the time to pay attention to other people's arguments won't fail to learn something from such arguments. People who are willing to learn, grow wiser.

Do you remember the day I attended the Academic Excellence Awards Ceremony at your school in 2017 at which you were honored for academic excellence together with about a hundred other students out of about three thousand students? Do you recall the most beautiful things each nominating teacher had written about each one of the recipients? Those comments were very touching and inspiring, indeed. But I observed that one of the key virtues that dominated the descriptions was, "He or she doesn't quit." I have also heard the same comment being said on other numerous occasions and settings.

Every time I hear that compliment, I feel that presenting, "not quitting," as one of the key characteristics of academic excellence and leadership, is to some extent, misleading. For me, quitting doesn't mean that one lacks the tenacity or mental stamina to hold on. But it means that one has the wisdom to discern and evaluate the situation at hand, has the grace to accept defeat, and the audacity to reframe one's ambitions. Sometimes, the failure to accept defeat or to quit may lead to unnecessary misery for oneself and others. This failure to quit may delay one's discovery of where his talents are. All my life, I have never been afraid to quit and perform a radical reorientation of my life. I have never regretted it.

My sons, when your situation is no longer workable, and you have tried your best to no avail, you should learn to retreat or even quit. Sometimes, the refusal to quit is a waste of time and resources. If your sound judgment tells you to quit, please, don't hesitate to quit. Many times, there is more wisdom in quitting than in persisting. However, you don't quit until you are convinced that it can do you better than persevering. Never quit prematurely.

At this juncture, the question you may want to ask, "How do I know when it's time to quit?" Unfortunately, there is no straight answer to your question. People are different, but you will be able to tell when it becomes unrewarding to continue pursuing than giving up. In most cases, giving up isn't a sign of cowardice. It's the brave and courageous who are ready to accept defeat and start afresh. It's the wise who know when they are defeated, and should quit. Please, quit, when you should. But never quit prematurely because that can be detrimental to your success.

My sons, if you opt for education, then you have to embrace the love of reading. Many people have committed their time to writing books so that those who are able, or wish to read may find the information that they require for their education. Nowadays, you also have educational information on the internet. Yes, you can play video games, listen to music, and watch movies, but that shouldn't be done at the expense of reading.

Don't just read the recommended books for your class, but you should read beyond that. A wider reader has a broader worldview. A worldview is a perspective through which one perceives and interprets the world. A larger worldview helps you to understand reality from many different perspectives. Learn to sacrifice some money in buying books. Indeed, the money used to buy books is never wasted.

You can also learn a great deal from life's experiences. This learning can only happen if you give yourself time to examine your experiences, and find out those things you would do differently if given another opportunity. My sons, learning from experiences isn't easy because life keeps changing the questions. When learning from experience, please, don't try to memorize the answers, but the formulae. If you memorize the answers, you would continue to fail the test because experiences are rarely repeated in the same way. You need to extract the wisdom out of life's experiences and use it to resolve new riddles of life.

Grab every opportunity to learn from your mistakes, if their very nature gives you the chance to learn. My sons, some errors, don't give you another chance to learn, so, avoid them. You should get inspiration from your successes. Learn from other people's experiences as well. Read books. Watch movies. Listen to stories. And learn.

You can also acquire an education through online studies. Online studies allow you the opportunity to pursue your other endeavors, and at the same time obtaining an academic qualification. Such educational programs enable you to educate yourself in the comfort of your home. However, online education demands utmost discipline, rigorous time management, and unwavering focus from the student. There are many people who have acquired academic and professional qualifications through that type of education. There are also people who tried that kind of education, and abandoned the programs half way though.

In any educational enterprise, my sons, discipline is the key. It's the undisciplined student who regularly misses homework deadlines, abscond from school, misses classes, listens to music while others are learning, and disrespects both the professor and other students. Utmost discipline is the key to success, my sons.

If you are given a choice between money and education, please, go for education because without it your money soon becomes the cause of your undoing. Or, go for both money and education because with money you can finance your educational expenses. With education, even if you don't have a job, you can still survive. With education, the sky can be the only limit you have. Don't forget that the world has become a global village, but it's the educated that can find a home anywhere in that village. The educated can live on the moon, and survive. The educated can turn a dry piece of land into some form of Paradise. The educated can change the direction of the flow of the water in a river. The educated can turn the wildest dreams into reality. Pursue education, my sons. A life lived in plenty but without knowledge, is a sad life.

My sons, when you obtain a plethora of educational accolades, never claim to know everything. You should have the humility to know the things that you know and leave others to know what they know. Never accumulate academic qualifications that you have never studied for because that will count heavily against you in life. Yes, many employers want to see your academic and professional certificates initially, but after that, what they want to see is the quality of your work.

People who claim to know more than they do, and masquerade as Jacks of all trades, aren't only hazardous to themselves, but also to their communities. If you give such people a piece of land to farm, they can turn it into a desert in one season. If you give them a wealthy country to rule, they can turn it into a basket case overnight. You give such persons a bank to run, the bank becomes bankrupt in a fortnight.

Don't mislead people by claiming to possess a plethora of academic achievements, but then fail to perform the tasks at hand to those people's satisfaction. In other words, an individual's level of education should be measured by the efficacy of his ideas and the quality of his work, not by the size and quantity of his academic certificates. I would rather employ an illiterate person who produces results, than a Jack of all trades who produces nothing.

My sons, you should know that there is no educational qualification that's better than the other. You might be a medical practitioner and get a higher salary than a theologian or carpenter, but that doesn't make a doctor's education better than the theologian's. You can't compare the knowledge of a medical practitioner and that of a theologian because they deal with different issues.

So, my sons, be educated in your area, and never think that you are better than other people who were trained in other fields. It's a shame that the society has chosen to award higher salaries for some professions over others, but that doesn't make such people more educated. If you want to compare people's education, you should do so with people that are in the same profession. Never feel professionally inferior. Learn to blossom where you are planted.

Yes, your academic regalia and certificates are important, but they might not be an accurate reflection of the knowledge and wisdom that you would have acquired. Let the fruits of your education speak for you. Don't just brag of your educational achievements unless you can use them. Education isn't reflected by the number of academic certificates that you hang on the walls of your office or home, but in the fruits of the work that you do. Unless a person who claims to be educated can show me what he or she has produced out of that education, to me he or she remains uneducated. Your studies must be reflected in those simple things you do every day. It must be seen in the choices you make, the people you associate with, the issues you discuss, the way you treat other human beings, and more so, the perspectives you use to interpret reality.

When you get educated, never look down on those people who didn't have the same educational opportunities as you did. You should remember that most of them didn't refuse to be educated. In fact, the world is full of wise people who didn't have as much educational opportunities as you have now. Don't laugh at people who can't write or read. Given a choice and a conducive environment, nobody would choose to be illiterate. Don't demean the people who aren't as fluent in foreign languages as you are. Fluence in a foreign language isn't a sign of intelligence, but of exposure. My sons, show kindness and tolerance for such people.

Never equate bookish education to wisdom. It's a good thing to be educated, but it's better to have wisdom, and it's best to have both knowledge and wisdom. In this world, you can lead a decent life if you have wisdom, but no formal education. But you can't survive if you have formal education and no wisdom. The uneducated are people too, and many times the educated have a lot to learn from them. So, my sons, grab every opportunity to get educated, use that knowledge, to gain a deeper and wider understanding of the world and its people. That's the beginning of wisdom, and you will live longer.

Enmity

Zino irema, rinosekerera newarisingadi (Some people can pretend to like you, when in fact, they are your enemies).
Chinokangamwa idemo, muti wakatemwa haukangamwi (The perpetrator can easily forget his or her wrongdoings, but the victim doesn't).

My sons, you can't be loved by everybody because it's unnatural, unnecessary, and unhealthy. This life won't only bless you with compassionate and caring friends, but also with enemies. There will be people who will hate you with a passion; some, for a cause, and others, for no apparent reason. Some people will just look at you, and then begin to dislike you. Just like that. Some people won't like the way you smile, talk, clothe, walk, or look at them. Some won't like the color of your skin. Some won't like the place where you live. Some won't approve of the people with whom you associate. Some will hate you for crossing their paths, which is inevitable in human relationships and encounters. Sometimes, people cross each other's path, either consciously or involuntarily.

Some people will hate you for stepping on their toes, or for your refusal to have them step on your toes. Some will hate you because of your success in life and at work, but others will hate you for lack of it. You will meet haters who just hate you for your generosity or lack of it. Some will hate you for speaking the truth to them and about them, or for hiding it from them. So, you must always remember that you can't be loved by everybody. A person who lives his life, works his job, cares for his beloved ones, speaks his mind, and observes his convictions, will always have someone who disagrees with him.

Enemies will always be there, and you must learn how to survive in their midst. Some people do survive by flight. However, at times, you can't flee your enemies because of the amount of power that they have, and the nature of your relationship with them. There are enemies who have more power than you have because of their political and financial status. If your enemy happens to be your boss or leader, it might not be possible to run away from him or her without disadvantaging yourself. You have to deal with them.

There are times when you can conquer your enemies by making them your friends. The adage says, "If you can't beat them, join them." You need to understand what they want from you and do it right, if possible. But, if what they require you to do is against your conscience and morality, then you should opt out, even if it means losing your job or position. You can't sacrifice what's right for a paycheck. You mustn't sacrifice your conscience for any amount of money because money comes and goes, but you will live with your conscience eternally. If your enemy is your boss, and if what he demands from you is against the laws of the land and your conscience, then you should opt out of that job.

If your enemy happens to be your neighbor, please, try to examine your conscience and find out what exactly makes him hate you. Our tendency is to blame others for our sour relationships with them. That's what humans do—blame others. Sometimes, people have genuine reasons for disliking us although we may not know those reasons. In any relationship that has gone bad, probe the part you might have played. Be sincere and non-judgmental. Make compromises if necessary, and your relationship will be restored. In friendship, there is no greater consolation than the restoration of a broken relationship. It's a sign of maturity and courage.

Of course, I know that you will meet antagonists who won't give you an opportunity to appease them, and I say, please, don't try. There are times when you must change your residence because your enemies can't be placated. It's better to resettle elsewhere than fight an unwinnable battle. At times, it's better to relocate than to wallow in an endless feud. Sell your house and buy another one in a different location. If you don't want to move, then erect a fence around your premises. They say that fences make good neighbors. But never fail to reconcile with those enemies that can be propitiated. Always seek to appease those that can be pacified. Avoid those that refuse to be mollified, lest you waste your time on them.

Sometimes your spouse becomes your enemy, and that's very unfortunate because it's against the principle of reciprocal love on which marriages are built. You should always know that when love turns into hatred, it burns like fire, and that fire is very difficult to put off. If that happens to you, please, get professional help as soon as possible. If professional intervention doesn't resolve the issues, you might consider opting out of the union. My sons, if you seek professional help, and there is no change in your relationship with your wife, divorce is the way. Don't impose yourself on any relationship because healthy relationships are built on mutual consent and love.

Women are beautiful people, and please, don't hesitate to find one who loves you. If you do, please, love her in return. Marry her, if she consents. But, when a woman's love turns to hatred, she hates with a passion. It's better to be a bachelor than live in a loveless relationship. Marriage is difficult even where the spouses reciprocate their love, and it's hell, where there is no love. If there is no more love left in a marriage, the honorable thing for you is to opt out. Never assume that your spouse has the same amount of love as you have, because that might not be the case. If your spouse is no longer interested in you, please, respect her feelings. But you should know that divorce isn't a piece of cake. It's a battle. It pierces the hearts of the couple involved. It demolishes the trust of the children and relatives. It endangers them. But when all is done to save a marriage to no avail, then divorce is the only way to sanity and wholeness. But it should be the last option.

Never allow your past marital challenges to prevent you from learning to love again. Of course, the scars of a broken relationship will remain with you forever. The smell of betrayal will always haunt you. The nightmares of the divorce battle will always tail you. But time heals. Yes, it does. But only if you allow it. The fact that you are nursing divorce wounds doesn't prevent other people from being attracted to you. Don't prevent them from showing their affection to you. Don't allow the wounds from your previous marriage to hold you captive for too long. Move on with life. Yes, some wounds heal with time, and others remain with us for life, but don't choose to be their slave. If given a choice between sadness and happiness, please, go for the latter because everyone of us deserves it.

There are innumerable reasons why there is hatred. I have met people who hate you because you stopped being nice to them. If you are a generous person, and then withdraw that generosity, its recipients might hate you for that. When the people you used to assist begin to hate you, it becomes more of a betrayal than hatred. These are people you would have supported in life, and probably made sacrifices for them.

Some people behave like little babies who are being weaned from their mothers' breast milk. I suppose that for some time, the weaned child hates its mother and father for depriving him of his most convenient and reliable source of nourishment. For every baby, being weaned from its mother's breast milk seems like betrayal of the highest order. But, for the parents, weaning a baby is a necessary part of human development. It must be done because no one can rely on breast milk for all eternity. Weaning, therefore, is a nasty experience for the baby, but also a very necessary one for its independence.

Weaning people from your generosity can be as unpopular just as weaning a baby from its mother's breast milk. The moment you say, "goodbye," some of them will turn into your enemies. If you are afraid of hatred, you will never be able to make them self-reliant. So, my sons, be generous to people, but when you feel that the time for them to fend for themselves has arrived, never hesitate to give them that opportunity. Some may hate you for it, but it's necessary for their self-reliance.

As for those people who hate you because you have offended them, please, try to make peace with them. Apologize and make up for your offense. Apologies heal. It's better to have an enemy who apologizes when wrong, than a friend who can't apologize. If you offend anybody, please, apologize. It's free. Some people will never ask you to pay reparations for the damage done, but will accept an apology from a humble and contrite heart.

Learn to say, "I am sorry." Be sincere in apologizing, but never demand forgiveness. Be haste to apologize, but never force the victim to forget the pain or scars caused by your actions. It's the responsibility of the offender to beg for forgiveness, but to forgive or not to forgive is up to the offended. That little phrase, "I am sorry," keeps this world alive. It makes nations avoid catastrophic wars. But don't apologize where you haven't done any wrong because that would be tantamount to committing suicide. You don't apologize just for the sake of it, but because that's the noble thing to do. If offended, please, don't force people to apologize because there is no value in an apology extracted from an offender by force.

Some people will dislike you for the person that you are. They are hated for the things that they can't change such as the color of their skin, facial looks, place of birth, and so on. Move on with your life. Don't apologize for being who you are. It's not a crime to look different, or to have a different personality. As long as you are doing what's right and lawful, be what you are. Let people love you for who you are, not because of what they want you to become. Life is too short to try to please everybody, because by the time you try to be yourself, it would be too late.

I have observed that sometimes love conquers all barriers that are caused by enmity. Some haters just need to be shown some love for them to change their perspectives about us. In Chicago, I worked under a supervisor, whose work ethic I considered unprofessional. My coworkers and I suspected her of backbiting and causing unnecessary firing of student workers. We thought that she didn't like student workers. Like most of my colleagues, I started hating her. This reciprocity of dislike went on for some time. I changed my attitude when one of my best friends was fired from work because of the negative reports that this lady had supplied to the director of the company. I knew that my turn of sorrow was also coming when the director told me that the supervisor was saying nasty things about me, behind my back. Although the manager assured me that he didn't believe her, I felt that I needed to do something about it.

I didn't want to lose my job because of her malicious gossip. I had to do something about it. I decided to give love a chance and it worked. One morning, as the lady arrived for work, I went to where she was, heartily greeted her, and offered her a friendly hug. She accepted, and I told her that I appreciated how she supervised us and was jubilant to assist her in any way necessary to make our company successful. I told her that she was a wonderful person. Of course, I didn't mean all that I confessed, but she bought it. She changed her attitude towards me. She became a friend. She even offered me transport back home whenever we finished work late at night. You know what, before I realized, I discovered that I meant everything that I said to her. What I considered my inauthenticity to her, transformed me. It turned my bitterness to acceptance. I began to see a very kind woman beneath her stern and cruel looks. My change of attitude also helped her to change her attitude.

Sometimes, we don't get along with other people just because we don't want to give love a chance. We are so convinced of our dislike of the other that we don't even try to change the way we treat or see such people. It's true, my sons, that at times, love conquers. Hatred breeds more hatred, and love begets love. When most of your energy is almost consumed by hate, please, try love.

Some haters just want to be appreciated, and that pacifies them. Sometimes, we are so much engaged in retaliation that we forget to see the kindness that lies beneath the corrections we receive from our bosses and presumed enemies. If the person who hates you is your subordinate at work, and you get to know about it, continue to respect him. Being fair and kind to such an employee may help him to appreciate your advice. Don't allow your knowledge of his hatred towards you to prevent you from seeing the good work that he does, and the sacrifices that he makes for the company. Do appreciate his work whenever necessary, and that may change him. There is power in showing your appreciation even for the little things that people do.

My sons, there are times when you have to confront your adversaries and fight them. You should learn to defend yourself and the people you love, from the onslaught of your foes. After pursuing all efforts to amicably resolve the issues that cause animosity between you and your enemies, stand your ground, and fight for what's right. Sometimes, there is no way out of animosity except that of firing back.

I used to run away from my adversaries until I discovered that some enemies could run faster than I. If you always run away from your enemies, you would end up having nowhere to run, for enemies are everywhere. If you should fight for your principles, please, don't hesitate. If you must defend what you believe in, please, stand your ground. However, it's unwise to fight unwinnable battles. You should know when to fight and what to fight for, but always pray for the wisdom of knowing when to run away for your life.

You need to learn to forgive, my sons. To forgive is to refuse to be imprisoned by one's past wounds. It's the willingness to start afresh despite the crippling setbacks suffered in the past. Forgiveness is an art that everyone should master because of several reasons. First, there are many times when those who do evil to you are so powerful that no one can bring them to justice. In some countries, some politicians and very wealthy people are above the law. The only way you can remain sane in such countries is by way of letting go.

Second, some wrongs that people do can never be undone through retaliation, compensation, or even imprisonment of perpetrators. The victim still needs to forgive in order to avoid remaining a prisoner of the past. Yes, perpetrators may be punished, but that doesn't bring automatic healing to your wounds. Third, forgiveness can be therapeutic because it shows that although your enemies have tried to dehumanize you, you still have the power to decide whether to forgive or not.

My sons, some evil people, will try to destroy you completely, but they can't take away your power to forgive them. Finally, forgiveness allows you to see both the perpetrator and you from a different perspective. Sometimes our perspectives influence the way we interpret what we see. Forgiveness can enable you to appreciate some of the good things that the wrongdoer does. You should remember that there are very few people who are completely evil—there is always a silver lining in every cloud.

My sons, in your quest to forgive, please, don't force your mind to forget the evil that would have happened to you because no one can consciously do that. Don't impose forgiveness on any individual. Allow your enemies to earn your forgiveness. Give them an opportunity to merit it. If they don't come to you begging for forgiveness, give it to them anyway, but just do it in your heart; silently. If you impose your forgiveness on people who have never asked for it, you are likely to deprive them of an opportunity to learn humility. Forgiveness, that is humbly earned, will be sincerely appreciated.

I encourage you to openly forgive perpetrators who ask for your forgiveness. But do it implicitly to those who don't request forgiveness. Don't give the unrepentant wrongdoer the benefit of the doubt; just forgive them in your heart. Don't tell them that you have forgiven them. It's good to forgive even those people who don't ask for it because some people don't know how to ask for forgiveness, or they don't have the humility to do it. After all, it's the sick that need a physician, not the healthy.

My sons, enemies will come and go, but continue to live your lives to the fullest. A man without enemies is a man without principles. He is like the salt that has lost its saltiness. Those who tenaciously stand by certain principles, will be opposed or hated for some of those principles. Don't allow hatred to stop you from being the man you are. Continue to be good. Sometimes, a man's character is measured by the number and caliber of his enemies. Those who fear enemies will live to dance according to other people's tunes. Speak your mind; stand by your principles; change your opinion if need be, and never lead someone else's life.

Cultural Diversity

Mwana waShe muranda kumwe (A person's position of privilege might not be recognized and respected in a foreign country).
Chitsva chiri murutsoka (A person who travels to new places, learns new things, and gets new opportunities).

My sons, you must know something about globalization and cultural diversity. Technological advancement has turned this world into a global village. It has made the movement of both people and information cheaper and faster. Now, people travel to places that they have never dreamt of visiting before. There is information everywhere. No country can easily control the kind of information that its population can read anymore. No country can remain an island any longer because the internet penetrates even borders built out of concrete walls.

When I was growing up, I used to be afraid of the dark. I dreaded the dark, not because the dark could bite me, but because of the wicked and mysterious witches who we believed took advantage of it. We believed that they plied their bewitching business in the cover of darkness, riding on hyenas, naked, and capable of entering even locked doors. Now, I think that the internet is more mysterious, pervasive, and intrusive than witches.

However, the internet, unlike witches, is mysterious in a positive way. Through the internet, people share their joys, tribulations, struggles, challenges, and successes. No one can suffer alone anymore. More people have access to information from all over the world. The strike of a key can take you to places that you have never imagined. From the internet, you can learn about other people, places, and job opportunities.

Zimbabweans too have taken advantage of the availability of information about other countries. Since the year 2000, many Zimbabweans have gone into the diaspora, running away from the economic meltdown that Zimbabwe has been experiencing, from which it's struggling to recover. Most people could do that because they had the information about where to go and how to get there.

It should be noted that getting information about where to go is one thing, and learning how to live in a foreign land is another. In the diaspora, people live as aliens among strangers. My sons, if you are to survive in a foreign land, you must learn the skills of interacting with people from other cultures. You should be interculturally informed.

My sons, you must realize that this world has people of different cultures, religions, political affiliations, and colors. Culture is the way people live their lives—the food they eat, the clothes they wear, the houses in which they live, the stories they tell, the music they sing, the dances and rituals they perform, the values they uphold, the art they make, and their understanding and interpretation of their experiences. Consequently, there are no people that have no culture. In addition to that, there is no culture that's superior to other cultures because all cultures are unique. A culture might look different to you, but that doesn't render it inferior or superior to yours.

My doctoral thesis supervisor contends that culture is like the human skin. Each person has a skin, and likewise, each person has a culture. The skin might be white, black, yellow or pink, but it's a skin. All skins are a mixture of smoothness and scars, but they are skins, and they effectively serve their purpose of protecting the human body. In the same manner, all people have cultures, and all cultures are a mixture of grace and sin. No culture is perfect, or entirely evil. All cultures are equally important although they are different. All cultures may seem weird and strange to an outsider. Never think that there is a culture that's superior to other cultures because there isn't. All cultures are different ways of living a life. You should always remember that your culture is as important as any other culture in the world. Never allow anybody to belittle it. Never worship other people's cultures at the expense of your own.

There is a tendency by people of all cultures to stereotype the people of other cultures. These generalizations may be positive or negative. My sons, don't use sweeping generalizations about other people, particularly if they are negative. Sweeping generalizations are blanket statements about individuals or things that tend to attribute some individual trait to the whole group without any evidence in support of that. Examples of such statements are: "All the Shona people are cowards." "The Ndebele people are violent." "All Zezuru people are intelligent." "All Shona people like peanut butter." "Americans are wise." Such stereotypes aren't only misleading, erroneous, and myopic, but also dangerous to both the speaker and the people they refer to.

An objective speaker is expected to know that good, evil, intelligent, or dull people are found among all ethnicities. There is no ethnicity that has a monopoly of any of these traits. Generalized statements lack the evidence which is needed to substantiate them because they are false most of the time. Such a mentality prevents the observer from evaluating each person as an individual, who might be different from other people of the same ethnicity.

Every person should be given an opportunity to prove his or her abilities and behavior, or a lack of them. A thief doesn't always give birth to a thief. A saint doesn't always give birth to a saint. Thievery and sainthood aren't passed on genetically. The fact that some Shona people are cowards doesn't make all of them cowards. The fact that Americans are wise, doesn't make all of them wise. Treat each person as an individual who is capable of molding her own character.

My sons, if you take to the habit of using sweeping statements about other people, you are likely to deprive yourself of the lessons and wisdom you can learn from others. Those who think that other ethnicities are unwise, are likely to deprive themselves of learning something from such ethnicities. Sweeping generalization only show the bigotry of the speaker. People should be judged as individuals, not groups. It's the individual that thinks, not the group.

My sons, cultures give their bearers an identity. Never run away from your own culture because it's like running away from yourself. If you do run away from your culture, the future would judge you harshly. Eat your cultural food wherever you are, if you can get it. But, the desire for your cultural diet shouldn't prevent you from eating and appreciating other people's foods. Sing your own songs wherever you are, if you still remember them, but that shouldn't prevent you from learning and enjoying other people's songs. Don't run away from your cultural names because they give you your identity. Acquire new names, but don't discard the cultural names.

Keep all the right practices of your culture, but don't deprive yourselves of learning from other cultures. Never feel guilty when you speak your vernacular language because there is nothing wrong about it. Learn and respect other languages, but don't deliberately forget yours. Encourage your children to be bilingual because it gives them an advantage over those people who speak only one language. He who forgets his culture loses his identity. Don't deprive your children of speaking their own language because they won't forgive you for that. There is nothing lost in understanding and speaking two or more languages, but the losses of not speaking one's vernacular are uncountable. The inability to speak one's own language renders one half dead.

I have been thinking about intercultural sensitivity and how it can be acquired. Those who have studied culture tell us that appreciating another culture isn't an easy thing to do. It's a process that demands one's deliberate effort of encountering and learning about the other. Using my own experience of living in the diaspora, I came up with the following *Intercultural Competence Development Stages* (ICDS).

Every intercultural learning begins with an encounter of the other. This encounter takes place in many ways such as, reading books and newspapers, watching movies, documentaries, and news, listening to stories, in classrooms or work places, and personal encounters. Most of the time, this encounter happens unintentionally. Sometimes, encounters with people of a different culture are inevitable, for they just happen. You get onto a bus, and you meet them. You turn on your television, and suddenly there is news about another culture. You get on a plane, and you find yourself sitting next to a person from a different culture. Thus, the encounter is the first stage in intercultural competence.

But the encounter alone can't help us acquire the skills that we need to interact respectfully and fruitfully with people of other cultures. Our reaction to that encounter is important. Some people become interested in learning more about the culture of the stranger. Other people suspect the other, and may become afraid. That fear may lead to the condemnation of the other's culture as not worth learning, or even stupid. Some people remain indifferent to the diverse cultural insights that might have come their way. It's the curious and adventurous who may get interested in learning more about a newly-encountered culture. This interest or curiosity is the beginning of intercultural sensitivity. If you want to change your perspective about other people, go out there, and meet them. You don't learn anything new about other cultures if you remain in your cultural comfort zone. You don't develop a new taste of food or music from other cultures if you don't try those foods or listen to other musical genres.

There are many people who haven't had a personal intercultural encounter. Most of the times, it's not their fault. The only stories they have heard about others are the negative ones. What's needed is to brave the winds by stepping out of one's cocoon and encounter others. There are also people who have encountered other cultures, but haven't developed a curiosity of understanding them deeply. Yes, it requires courage to be able to develop that curiosity. My sons, if you want to learn the skills of living interculturally, take the risk to go out, and encounter the other. There are people waiting to connect with you, but only if you take the risk of encountering them.

The initial encounter lays the foundation for further exploration of the other culture, but might not be sufficient for the development of intercultural sensitivity. Once one becomes aware of the existence of another culture, the second stage is to seek further exploration of that particular culture to acquire more knowledge about it. Most people who look down on other cultures don't do so because of the things they know about other cultures, but because of their ignorance of those cultures. They blow the little they know out of proportion. Usually, the little they know are negative stereotypes that are reinforced by fear of the other.

My sons, the encounter alone isn't good enough, learn more about the encountered culture. You can only appreciate what you know, and not what you don't know. To deepen your knowledge of other cultures, watch documentaries, read books, talk to people, take a class, visit other places, and so on. Of course, the acquisition of this knowledge may be used either positively or negatively. Some people, armed with the facts, may use such knowledge to segregate or discriminate against those cultures. On the other hand, some people begin to respect other cultures because they know more about them. Constructive knowledge should lead to praxis.

My sons, the third stage in the development of intercultural sensitivity is the cultivation of empathy for the encountered culture. Empathy means the ability to stand in another person's shoes and try to feel the way she feels in being a member of her cultural group. This stage begins with a deliberate move to look at the other culture objectively. This objectivity is a result of one's humility and compassion for others, and the awareness that no culture is perfect.

It calls the one learning about another culture to set aside his preconceived ideas about the culture in question. It also calls for a genuine hunt for the positive from the other. This positive attitude doesn't seek to sweep the bad aspects of the other culture under the carpet, but it's a strategy to conquer the negative stereotypes that we might have read or heard about the other. One has to try to interpolate this new culture with his own cultural practices. This interpolation helps the inquirer to identify the similarities between his culture and the encountered culture.

Empathy for the other breeds respect for him. Respect doesn't mean the total acceptance of the other culture, but the celebration of the graces in that culture and the acknowledgement of the differences. This celebration of the graces and acknowledgment of the differences are the permission for the other person to live his culture without the fear of being judged, condemned, and ostracized. Respect of a culture leads to the respect of the person who practices that culture. Usually, this respect is reciprocated by the other person.

This appreciation of otherness empowers and humanizes the other person who might have been disempowered and dehumanized because of his otherness. Sometimes, one's otherness imprisons him and stifles all his talents. To respect a stranger and his culture is to reaffirm the humanity of every human being. It compels the other to get involved in the new culture with the knowledge that his own culture isn't condemned. It encourages the other to try new food, learn the new language, make new friends, and listen to new music and stories, without having the feeling of betraying his own.

The final and most difficult stage in developing intercultural sensitivity is integration. Integration is the bringing together of different cultures to have equal participation in society and its institutions. Integration involves taking the risk of trusting the other. It entails the wisdom to know that having a different accent doesn't mean that one is less intelligent. Integration calls for the acceptance of the other into our schools, work places, churches, and even homes. This acceptance requires the trust that the accepted person would deliver the skills for which he is hired.

Integration may entail worshiping the same God together albeit in different languages, listening to different kinds of music but still getting inspired, and eating different foods, but still getting nourishment. It's the realization that the other is human too, with his graces and sins, and struggles and victories, just like us. It brings the other into our own homes, and accepting invitation to his own. It may lead to intercultural marriages. It allows us to acquire multiple perspectives through which to understand and interpret reality. It drives away all the fear that we might have of the other, for it demystifies the negative stereotypes that we have.

A culturally integrated society is the society of the future. No one can run away from globalization. The world needs interculturally integrated society. A society where every member can contribute to the wellbeing of the society regardless of his cultural identity.

(Note: *The above stages have been inspired by Milton J. Bennett's Developmental Model of Intercultural Sensitivity.*)

My sons, if you become the manager of any company or institution, don't hire employees according to their nationalities, but according to their abilities. If there is a stranger, who is qualified to do the job, give him the opportunity to show you what she can do. Don't give a job to a relative who doesn't know how to do it, for it destroys the company. Find other ways of assisting your friends and relatives, but give the job to the person who is qualified to do it. In fact, you should try to give your ear to the stranger because she has a new way of interpreting and understanding reality. A stranger has new stories and theories that you have never heard before. A visitor can help you see things from a different angle, and perhaps more clearly than before, if you have time to listen.

Wherever you go, try to represent your nation. Be the ambassador of your people. Don't tarnish your people's image. Don't behave in a manner that would bring disrepute upon all the people who come from your country. Work hard. Be honest. Smile. Respect people. In fact, behave in a way that even if someone were to tell your superiors lies about you, the superiors wouldn't believe him.

So, my sons, respect your identity, while allowing yourselves to learn from other cultures. Don't hesitate to teach others about your culture, if they give you an opportunity to do so. But be ready to learn other people's cultures. You should always remember that although people belong to different ethnicities, they remain individuals who deserve to be respected. If given a choice, please, embrace cultural integrations.

Summing it up

My sons, I don't claim to have the panacea for all the challenges that you will encounter in this life. These guidelines aren't intended to be inviolable biblical truths on which you should base your lives. I don't doubt the capacity of every human being to manufacture his own wisdom, for people are unique. These guidelines reflect how I view life, and what I have learnt from my own life experiences. You have the right to be a student of your own life experiences, and define your own destiny. I won't begrudge you if you become wiser than I.

This piece of advice challenges you not to act impetuously, but to stop and think before you act. My views may sound very old-fashioned because I belong to an older generation, but are helpful all the same. Remember, not everything that's old-fashioned is useless. Look at how old-fashioned the air we breathe is, but those who are arrogant and too modern to forgo breathing, will lose their modern lives. Take from this piece what you think is necessary, and discard what is impractical. This writing might seem erudite for you now, but there shall come a time when you will look at it and find it wanting. Open your eyes and ears and learn from whoever is kind enough to teach you something. Whatever you do, wherever you go, desire to manufacture your own wisdom.

www.ingramcontent.com/pod-product-compliance
Lightning Source LLC
Chambersburg PA
CBHW030907170426
43193CB00009BA/763